THE CANADIAN KINGS OF REPERTOIRE

The Story of the Marks Brothers

160201

Michael V. Taylo

NATURAL HERITAGE/NATURAL HISTORY INC.

The Canadian Kings of Repertoire: The Story of the Marks Brothers
Michael V. Taylor

Published by Natural Heritage/Natural History Inc.
P.O. Box 95, Station O, Toronto, Ontario M4A 2M8

National Library of Canada Cataloguing in Publication Data

Taylor, Michael V.
    The Canadian kings of repertoire : the story of the Marks Brothers

Includes bibliographical references and index.
ISBN 1-896219-76-4

1. Marks Brothers. 2. Theatrical companies—Canada—History. I. Title.

PN2308.M37T39 2001   792.2'028'092271   C2001-902444-4

Cover, illustrations and text design by Derek Chung Tiam Fook
Edited by Jane Gibson
Printed and bound in Canada by Hignell Printing Limited, Winnipeg, Manitoba.

Natural Heritage / Natural History Inc. acknowledges the financial support of the Canada Council for the Arts and the Ontario Arts Council for our publishing program. We also acknowledge the financial support of the Government of Canada through the Book Publishing Industry Development Program (BPIDP) and the Association for the Export of Canadian Books.

"The world wants to laugh above all else
and the man who can consistently sell tickets
to a real side-shaking giggle
is a benefactor on the road to fortune."

R.W. Marks
1921

TABLE OF CONTENTS

FOREWORD

Each year at the Perth Museum we present exhibitions that are related to some aspect of Perth's history. When Barry Penhale, publisher of Natural Heritage Books called in the fall of 2000 to tell us about the upcoming publication of this book on the Marks Brothers, we were truly excited and inspired to create an exhibition on the history of theatre and entertainment in Perth over the years. Using artifacts from our own collection and others on loan from local theatre groups, avid collectors and historians, we are presenting the exhibition "On Stage in Perth" during the summer of 2001 to celebrate the launch of this book.

There is a long and unique history of theatre in this town dating back to the mid 19th century. The era of the fabulous Marks Brothers is one of the most exciting stories in our colourful past. They have been called "the most remarkable theatrical family in Canadian history. The dazzling Marks Brothers were the greatest impresario-performers of our small town stage in the era before the nickelodeon." (*Maclean's Magazine*, 1958).

The Marks Brothers troupes performed all over Canada and the United States for fifty years from the 1870s to the 1920s. They delighted audiences in many remote towns and villages, most of them starved for entertainment, with their flamboyant performances and lavish scenery.

Each year, after 40 weeks on the road, they would return to their home base, a farm on the shore of Christie Lake, close to Perth. There they would rehearse, relax and plan the next seasons' performances. The silk-hatted Marks Brothers were larger than life and when they came home to Perth everyday existence would suddenly become more exciting.

By the mid-1920s, vaudeville acts and roadshows were declining in popularity and, with the last performance of the Marks Brothers Dramatic Company, came the end of an era. But the Marks Brothers have never been forgotten here in Perth. Over the years, several local theatre

groups have dusted off the old scripts taken from the Perth Museum archives, and held Marks Brothers revivals.

In 1982, Theatre-on-the-Tay presented "The Duke's Daughter," the first of three plays. The Marks Brothers revival continued the next year with their performance of "Dolores, the Ranch Queen" and in 1984 came "Dora Thorn." The program for "Dora Thorn" described the ingredients of the play in this manner – "the dashing young protagonist, the innocent heroine and their struggle to fulfill their love amidst prejudice and deception. To say that in the end love conquers all is not to spoil the ending for anyone, for in melodrama getting there is all the fun."

In the fall of 2000, the theatre group Barndoor Productions put on the Marks Brothers play "The Wolf," a melodrama of the Hudson Bay Country. They are hoping to produce more in the future.

It is fitting that Michael Taylor tackled the project of writing a book on the Marks Brothers. Michael was editor of the *Perth Courier* for several years and had a deep interest in the history of this area and researched his subject matter thoroughly. This book will introduce readers to this important part of our theatrical history. The Marks Brothers and their theatrical legacy deserve to be recognized and remembered.

Susan McNichol
Curator, Matheson House, Home of the Perth Museum

Robert William, better known as R.W., the eldest of the seven Marks Brothers, had a "head for business" and a natural theatrical bent. It was his acumen and his imagination that initiated and established the Marks Brothers theatrical troupes as the possibly best known performers of their time. *Perth Museum Collection*

CHAPTER 1

HOW ARE YOU GOING TO KEEP THEM DOWN ON THE FARM? – 1876 TO 1882

"Listen! Folks! Listen!" So went the ballyhoo of King Kennedy, magician, the "Mysterious Hindu from the Bay of Bengal," as he motioned a small and inattentive crowd to step closer and view first-hand the never-before-seen mysteries of the Orient.

King Kennedy was a lot of things, but a Hindu from the distant shores of Pakistan, he was not. In fact, the only border he ever crossed was between Canada and the United States. He was, in reality, an itinerant showman, and not a very successful one at that, as was evidenced by the apathetic reception he was receiving from the assemblage in the small Eastern Ontario hamlet of Maberly.

Kennedy's banter reverberated around the village well over one hundred years ago. Like his many contemporaries, he toured the Canadian hinterland during the post-Confederation period, entertaining audiences with card and slight-of-hand tricks, ventriloquism stunts and popular songs.

As the crowd gingerly edged its way closer to the gesticulating "Hindu" on that crisp autumn evening of 1876, a nineteen-year-old youth named Robert William Marks, purveyor of sewing machines and five-octave harmonicas, took stock of the less than enthusiastic gathering and attributed its apathy to the magician's mediocre performance. But luckily for the "Mysterious Hindu," Robert Marks (R.W.) recognized the native cleverness of the performer and fixed a conclusion in his mind: that King Kennedy, properly managed, could generate three times the gate receipts. According to popular belief at the conclusion of the evening's performance, R.W. approached Kennedy with a proposition:

"I own a team of horses and a wagon; you have a tent and a lot of clever bunco. Let's hitch and take fifty-fifty of the profits."[1]

Thirty-six years later, however, R.W. would give a less fictional account of this historic meeting:

"One night, in the company of several other young men I went to the village of Maberly to an entertainment put on by a magician and ventriloquist. The show was all right but the men were evidently travelling in hard luck. After the show I asked them what they would ask for a week's engagement. They would not sell it out for a week, but offered me half interest in the show at a low price and I took them up. I knew a number of good villages in that locality, and with my father's democrat and horses I started on the road with the company. I made money right from the start, and the next season had control of the company myself."[2]

From that day on R.W. never looked back. It was this chance meeting that formed the foundation of the famous Marks Brothers travelling theatrical companies, which, from its humble beginnings of one company in 1876, mushroomed into four independent troupes by the turn of the century. The Marks brothers, born of Irish-Canadian parents in rural Lanark County were seven in all: Robert William, generally known as R.W., Tom, John, Joseph, Alex, McIntyre (usually called Mack) and Ernie. With the exception of John, one by one they left the family farm at Christie Lake, near Perth, Ontario, and "took to the boards." Their sisters, Nellie (Ellen Jane) and Libby (Olivia Mariah), never appeared on stage and by all accounts never aspired to do so.

Although R.W. had no theatrical experience whatsoever when the glare of kerosene footlights captured his imagination, he did, however, have enough savvy to learn quickly how to please the entertainment-starved populace of the day. When Tom, the second oldest (b.1857) joined R.W.'s fledgling company circa 1879, history records he willingly abandoned his apprenticeship to a local cobbler. However, an article in the October 1, 1926, issue of *Maclean's* magazine tells a different story. The author, James A. Cowan, had interviewed Tom at his Christie Lake home earlier that year. According to this article, the aging actor had already had considerable show business experience – experience gained while touring throughout the United States with Buffalo Bill Cody and a number of blackface minstrel shows before joining his brother. It is highly unlikely that this was the case, as extensive research on the subject has failed to uncover any factual information to substantiate this claim. Notwithstanding, Tom's earlier exploits as recounted by Cowan make interesting reading.

Alex (b. 1867) was the next in line to contract "stage fever." Without hesitation, he traded his pitchfork for a silver-headed cane and joined his celebrated brothers. Joe (b. 1861) was within six months of becoming an ordained Anglican minister when the lure of the "kerosene circuit" and the charms of a pretty *soubrette* convinced him his future lay in a different direction. When Ernie, the youngest (b. 1879), added his name to the Marks Brothers playbill, he had already left high school and was apprenticing as a cheesemaker in a small factory on Concession 3 of Bathurst township. But it was not until after the turn of the century that Mack (b. 1871) finally capitulated and donned the top hat, tails and diamonds that distinguished the Marks Brothers from all other troupes in their out-of-door appearance. John, the third oldest (b. 1859) had very little to do with the theatrical exploits of his brothers. He, like his sisters, never appeared on the stage, but it is believed he acted as advance agent on occasion before moving to the western United States in 1886 to seek his fortune in an unrelated line of work.

R.W. and King Kennedy were, at first, content to play the numerous town halls, hotels, fraternity houses and church halls that abounded throughout rural Eastern Ontario. But after several years of performing their mixed bill of music, magic, card tricks, jokes and ventriloquism stunts, and meeting with only limited success, they decided a change of venue might broaden their horizons. Thus, a decision was made to embark on an extended road tour which would have its beginnings in Western Canada.

In the spring of 1879, R.W. and Kennedy began their sojourn to Winnipeg. [According to an article in the *Perth Courier* of August 27, 1937, Tom left for Winnipeg with R.W. and King Kennedy in 1879. There are differing accounts of when and how Tom Marks joined his brother's theatrical company.] Getting there would prove to be a monumental task as it would still be another six years before the transcontinental Canadian Pacific Railway would be completed. Necessity dictated they should make their way to Northern Ontario by horse and buggy where they would catch a west-bound train. This slow, but dependable mode of transportation also served an alternative purpose as it allowed the company, such as it was, to play one-night stands in the numerous communities that dotted the route. They were thereby guaranteed a consistent source of income which would enable them to bring their specialized brand of entertainment to the early settlers of the West. In later years, R.W. would recall:

> "We drove the team and buggy to Owen Sound and then boarded the 'Northern Belle' to Parry Sound, then it was on to Copper Cliff, Manitoulin Island and Port Arthur. I could have vaulted across Winnipeg

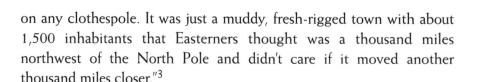

on any clothespole. It was just a muddy, fresh-rigged town with about 1,500 inhabitants that Easterners thought was a thousand miles northwest of the North Pole and didn't care if it moved another thousand miles closer."[3]

Winnipeg, may not have been quite as rustic as R.W. described it, for, despite his unflattering remarks, the settlement one year later was a hive of activity as the following narrative recounts:

"We saw a broad main street boarded with high wooden sidewalks and rows of shops of every shape and size. Some were rude wooden shanties, others were fine buildings of yellow brick. High over all towered the handsome spire of Knox Church. Several saw and grist mills sent up incessant puffs of white steam into the clear air. The street was full of bustle and life. There were wagons of all descriptions standing before the stores. Long lines of Red River carts were loading with freight for the interior.

"The sidewalks were filled with a miscellaneous crowd of people: – German peasants, French half-breeds, Indians, Scots and English people, looking as they do all the world over. The middle of the street, though there had not been a single drop of rain, was a vast expanse of mud – mud so tenacious that the wheels of the wagons driving through it were almost as large as mill-wheels, and when we dared to cross it, we came out the other side with much difficulty, and feet of elephantine proportions.

"The city of Winnipeg, which eight years ago was nothing more than a cluster of houses about the Hudson's Bay Company's fort now contains 7,000 inhabitants."[4]

Having reached their destination, R.W. immediately set about finding a suitable location in which the company could "demonstrate their wares." One was found, but not in the town hall or opera house as might be expected, but in one of the numerous smaller halls that were common place in Western communities. These buildings were usually extensions of local bars and saloons. One of these establishments was the Pride of the West Saloon, which was "proud of its piano, and supported a high class vaudeville."[5] Red River Hall was Winnipeg's first theatre, built in 1871. The stage , consisting of a platform raised about a foot off the floor, was lighted by oil lamps and heated by several stoves. The only entrance and exit was a narrow plank staircase running transversely across one end of the building on the outside. Other makeshift theatres soon followed: Theatre Royal, Dufferin Hall and the Winnipeg Opera House. When Cool Burgess arrived in 1877, Winnipeg became a regular attraction for professional touring companies.

R.W. never mentioned where the company actually played its first Winnipeg performance. Perhaps it was in the Pride of the West Saloon, but we do know they played for three nights and those burly patrons without ready cash to pay their admission did so with gold dust.

Up until the time of his death in 1936, R.W. maintained their show was the first organized entertainment of its type ever to perform in Winnipeg. The *Winnipeg Free Press*, as it was then, helped substantiate this claim by declaring, "Hurrah, we're not in the backwoods anymore, a show has come to town."[6] On reading this excerpt, Winnipeg residents would have, no doubt, recalled other professional touring companies that had performed in the community prior to the arrival of R.W. and Kennedy, performers such as E.A. McDowell and Cool Burgess. When Burgess played the town in 1877, the *Free Press*, conscious of this significant event, had commented: "The visit of the first professional troupe to this province will long be remembered as an interesting era in the social history of Winnipeg."[7]

Regardless of which troupe was first, the "wandering minstrels" from Lanark County, it is said, performed admirably, even though seating arrangements left much to be desired. In order to watch the production in relative comfort, many patrons were forced to sit on beer and nail kegs and rough planking. R.W. never said whether or not the engagement was a financial success, but the following quotation lends one to believe that it was not that lucrative a venture:

"We weren't looking for money, we wanted experience and we got it."[8]

Winnipeg had not only provided R.W. with the experience he had been seeking, but it was also an ideal point from which to embark into the more populated and affluent towns of the American midwest. The only efficient mode of transportation into the Dakota Territories from Manitoba in those days was the "flyer" or flat-boat down the Red River. With their newly-found confidence, R.W. and Kennedy, accompanied by three or four hardy individuals who had signed on to assist the budding troupe, wasted no time in taking to the boats.

Their first, although unscheduled, stop in this new territory was at Grand Forks, North Dakota. No sooner had the "flyer" slipped into the wharf, when the town sheriff, fingering a holstered revolver, made his appearance. After dispensing with the customary greetings and salutations, the peace officer, upon learning of their profession refused to allow the thespians to continue their journey and ordered them ashore. R.W. was at a loss to explain the reason for the lawman's seemingly hostile attitude, but as it turned out no malice was intended. All that was required of the company in order to continue its trek was to give a performance.

> "The townspeople won't let you go," stated the lawman.
> "But you have no hall," protested R.W. as he surveyed the settlement from the jetty.
> "If you give the order, we'll fix up an opera house in half an hour," came the sheriff's ready reply.[9]

Realizing the futility of declining this obvious attempt at extortion, R.W. reluctantly consented to give one performance and one performance only. Within minutes of R.W. having declared his intentions, half the able-bodied men in town were scurrying about collecting beer kegs, planks and tables, which were then set-up in a yet unfinished store, and instantly transformed it into an "opry house." What had initially began as an impromptu entertainment stretched into a three-performance engagement. Yet this was not the first organized entertainment Grand Forks had ever seen, as one might expect considering the circumstances. Several years earlier, residents had attended a production of "Only a Farmer's Daughter," and had been incensed at the format because it poked fun at a rural community. The local newspaper announced grimly that no more such offerings would be tolerated.[10]

Whenever a touring troupe struck town in the American West during the 1880s, cast members risked acquiring a perforated hide, thanks to the antics of pistol-packing cowboys who delighted in shooting out the footlight chimneys. The unofficial mandate of most towns during this period decreed all itinerant companies should be the natural target of the drunken, well-armed cow-puncher. These overt acts of hostility, performed under the guise of "good fun" invariably reduced the house to darkness and chaos within minutes, and proved very disconcerting to the more respectable patrons in the audience. But more importantly, this form of horseplay was eating into R.W.'s profits. Touring troupes were responsible for all property damage incurred during a performance, and this fact alone deemed it necessary to devise a quick and affordable solution to the dilemma.

R.W. was obviously one those rare individuals endowed with the uncanny ability to assess a situation and act accordingly, giving little regard to the consequences. His ultimate solution in solving this problem had a touch of genius about it – simply hire the local ruffians to police each performance, thereby ensuring their continued pacification for the duration of the company's engagement. Implementing this idea was as simple as the solution itself. R.W. would leave the troupe on the outskirts of town while he made his way to the local saloon. Here he would enquire of those individuals known to delight in the sport of "chimney potting" or any other disruptive activity. Then, with names in hand he would seek them out and, once found, the combination of his ready Irish wit, bawdy conversation and more than a liberal amount of drink, would result in an understanding they were to enter his employ as peacekeepers for the duration of the show.

In theory, this somewhat novel approach should have worked, and to some degree it did. But there were other unforeseen ramifications that would soon make themselves apparent. With solemn conscientiousness these defenders of law and order carried out their appointed task. Ugly and burly, they would patrol the aisles during the performance, swaggering from left to right under the influence of R.W.'s whiskey. Woe betide the man or woman who laughed at the wrong cue or laughed too loud. Within seconds of the outburst, one of the ruffians would appear, tap the miscreant on the shoulder and mumble something about "filling them full of lead." R.W., the consummate businessman and manager that he was, had succeeded in applying a "band-aid solution" to the problem, but some years later he would reflect upon the wisdom of his actions by saying:

"The gunmen kind'a, spoiled the quiet scenes."[11]

R.W.'s imposing stature, for he stood just over six feet and was impressively broad-shouldered, demanded a modicum of respect, and this was generally accorded him in most villages and towns throughout the Dominion and the northern United States. But such was not always the case in the American midwest, where the motto, "God created man, but Samuel Colt made them equal," was the catchword of the day. Caldwell, Kansas, in the early 1880s could aptly be described as one such typical western town of the period. This was a town where whiskey and bullets went hand in hand and a six-gun did the talking for most men.

A story is told that no sane individual would dare wear a plug topper while strolling about town for fear of the obvious consequences. But R.W. then, and until the time of his death, always wore a silk top hat – a trademark that distinguishes the Marks Brothers from all other troupes in their public appearances. When warned of the impending danger awaiting him should he fail to remove his *chapeau*, R.W., in typical fashion, threw all caution to the wind and marched down the main street to the Silver Dollar Hotel. Once inside he took note of his surroundings and sat down. But as soon as his feet touched the floor, he detected a solemn footfall behind him. In an instant, a pistol was lodged within inches of his "topper." Just as quickly the crack of two bullets echoed around the room before they found their way into the opposite wall. Understandably, R.W. was somewhat shaken by this incident, but with poise and dignity befitting royalty, he turned, faced the gunman and said, "Pardner, please take better aim next time."

With smoking gun in hand, the cowboy glowered above him, stunned by R.W.'s cool and calculated manner. The wrangler in his half-drunken stupor had mistaken the actor for a preacher. When he realized his error, he blurted, "Will ya trade hats?" R.W., caught off-guard by this unusual request, hesitated for a moment. Fortunately he caught the attention of a gesticulating bartender who had taken cover behind a partition when the shooting started, urging him to accept the proposal. Without further ado, R.W. declared, "Done!" In the true spirit of the West the deal was consummated with round after round of drinks. As luck would have it, this incident proved most opportune for R.W as the wrangler was one of the largest ranchers in the area. To show his admiration for the itinerant showman, he ordered a number of his ranch hands to form a guard of honour and escort the Canadian about town. He also declared that each of his employees must purchase at least one ticket for the evening's performance.[12]

As early as 1881, R.W. began formulating a long range plan for the company. During his trek through the American West he had encountered a number of troupes who were performing a similar style of entertainment, but in a more polished manner. These companies had included in their repertoire the usual variety players, but augmented the playbill with one and two act melodramas which were well-received by the theatre-going public. R.W. realized that if the company failed to keep pace with the ever-increasing standards demanded by audiences, the troupe would inevitably fall victim to what many considered the showman's death rattle – mediocrity.

He had no intention of descending into that chasm, an abyss from which few entertainers ever emerged. Instead, he initiated a plan of action that would ensure the company's continued success. By now, he had recruited his brother Tom to replace King Kennedy (who had left the troupe for parts unknown) and combined their talents with two Kansas *soubrettes*, Emma Wells and her sister Jennie, who took the stage name of Jennie Ray. For many years, it was generally accepted that a chance meeting in Caldwell led to this union; but in 1932, R.W. refuted this belief:

"In Pittsburgh, in 1882, two ladies were added to the company."[13]

The lovely Emma Wells, vocalist and leading lady, joined R.W. and Tom Marks in 1882, along with her sister Jennie Ray, to form the touring company then known as "The Big Four." The photograph was taken by the W. Bogart Studio of Newmarket, Ontario, date unknown. *Perth Museum Collection.*

Jennie Ray, pianist and sister of Emma Wells, was the fourth member of the early troupe that would become the Emma Wells Concert Company. She remained with the troupe until about 1890. *Perth Museum Collection.*

The newly formed troupe specializing in variety was known as " The Big Four."

In the ensuing years it came as no surprise that their business relationship should blossom into one of a more personal nature. R.W. and Emma Wells remained *paramours* for sixteen years, while Tom and Jennie Ray ended their rumoured liaison about 1885, prior to his marrying Ella Maude Brokenshire, of Wingham, Ontario. As the company's reputation grew, R.W. was cognizant that "appearances" had to be maintained, so in keeping with Victorian attitudes of the day, he let it be known that the ladies from Kansas were in fact – his cousins. This ploy was intended to appease the more sensitive and moralistic segment of society who would look upon such an "un-Godly" liaison with utter disdain and condemnation.

Under normal circumstances, this deception would have been unnecessary had the company remained content to play strictly variety. Scattered throughout the West were thousands of communities whose inhabitants were not overly concerned as to the purity and righteousness of their entertainers or their entertainment. But R.W. had the foresight to realize there was a relatively untapped audience waiting in the wings — an audience comprised mainly of women and children who seldom, if ever, had the opportunity to attend a performance given by a travelling company for fear of having their Puritan sensibilities damaged beyond repair. Ultimately, it was this faction of the population that R.W. wanted to reach; their numbers were in the hundreds of thousands if not millions, and common sense dictated even at five cents "a head," there was a fortune to be made by catering to this, the silent majority, who wanted only to see wholesome, family entertainment. As R.W. noted in a 1921 interview:

> "There are two kinds of people we try to draw, the young man and his girl who want to see every show end with a marriage, and the middle-aged, unromantic team of house-keepers who look on marriage as a chestnut and want to see some of the tragedy and clash of fiction. Then, of course, everybody, young and old, or middle-aged, loves a comedy. The comedian's jest is the great universal tonic. Above everything else the world wants to laugh, and the man who can sell tickets to a laugh is on his way to fortune."[14]

In the same interview R.W. outlined some basic show business philosophy:

> "The best time to go into a town with a show is immediately after the declaration of a strike. The average workman meets his chum; 'Bill,' says he, 'we're going to win this strike. 'Right you are,' says Bill, 'and in two

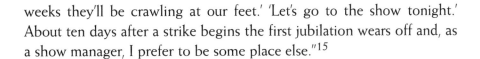

weeks they'll be crawling at our feet.' 'Let's go to the show tonight.' About ten days after a strike begins the first jubilation wears off and, as a show manager, I prefer to be some place else."[15]

"The Big Four," with its expanded repertoire, decided the time had come to embark on a cross-country tour in order to enlarge its growing "sphere of influence." According to Tom, in a 1921 interview with *Maclean's* magazine, the company headlined with great success in most major cities from San Francisco to New York. Along the way they entertained the inhabitants of small-town America, and some communities were so small they could not even lay claim to being a "one-horse" town. But the rough and tumble mining and logging towns offered the company its greatest challenges.

Somewhere along the route the troupe underwent a name change. "The Big Four" had passed into oblivion, and in its place emerged the "Emma Wells Concert Company." The Emma Wells Concert Company was exactly what its name implied, a company that offered the intelligent public a varied and refined entertainment, combining the best of the old favourites with new innovations and melodrama.

R.W. was forever destined to play the straight man, while Tom, a natural comedian, served as comedy lead. Their jokes culled from the pages of old almanacs and similar publications were simple but effective:

> R.W.: "Can't understand that hen of mine. Everytime I see her she's sitting on an axe."
> Tom : "She's broody, you fool. She's only trying to hatchet!"

and

> Tom: "So you're a college man, are you?"
> R.W.: "Yes indeed. I have studied Latin, Greek, geometry and algebra."
> Tom: "All right, if you're so smart, let's hear you say it's a fine day in algebra."[16]

But prior to assuming their on-stage roles, R.W. and Tom had other tasks to perform – equally important; they were obliged to divide between them the duties of doorman and ticket-taker. Emma Wells was also remarkable in her own right. She would soon gain nation-wide fame for her four-voiced vocalisms, which entailed singing in rapid succession, soprano, alto, tenor and bass. As well, she was an accomplished pianist and dancer.

The American logging and mining towns of the 1880s and 1890s would prove to be a financial boon to those adventurous stock companies. Not only did they endure verbal abuse, but more often than not risked personal injury at the hands of whiskey-soaked roughnecks who prided themselves on their ability to disrupt an evening's performance at the "drop of a hat." It was a rare occasion indeed, when R.W. and Tom were not called upon to forcibly eject at least one boisterous member of the audience for his unsolicited "stage participation." In essence, this nightly ritual amounted to "theatrical warfare." Theirs was a never-ending crusade to ensure peace and quiet, and their subsequent success in maintaining law and order earned them enormous respect.

Their highly efficient method of ejection was technically known as "going over the footlights." The skill acquired by these two Lanark County farmboys made it a simple process, requiring only a few minutes of a man's time. Whenever it became apparent that a spectator was a chronic interrupter, one or both of the brothers, accompanied by as many members of the company as was deemed necessary to handle the situation, would leap into the house and whisk the miscreant into the street. With matters well in hand the performance would continue, confident that no further interruptions would be forthcoming that night. Many evenings while R.W. and Tom were busy with their extra curricular activities, the remaining cast members would continue the production, awaiting the return of the "battling duo." Upon completion of their task, the two would leap back on stage and resume where they had left off, as if nothing had happened.

Some years later, Tom would say that the Pennsylvania mining towns, Mississippi settlements and the raw Montana communities offered the biggest challenge.[17] Whenever the company played these hostile territories, R.W. and Tom literally fought their way through each performance. Yet, this necessary, but regrettable, activity quickly endeared them to the more sedate patrons, who endowed upon them the nickname, "the strongman and the wildcat." These Lanark County natives were credited at the time, so the literature suggests, with changing the whole complexion of show business in these areas. The rowdy element accounted for a very small percentage of the total population, but its consistent trouble-making had kept respectable citizens away from the theatres. The peace-loving segment of society had no intention of paying for an evening's entertainment only to become embroiled in a near riot.

"The strongman and the wildcat" squelched these disturbances without mercy, and their reputations were well known all over the continent to both showmen and ruffian alike. During these "blood and thunder" days, they forged their pugilistic reputations in stone and sinew, as more than one aching and bruised heckler would attest after he found himself tossed out on his ear, accompanied by a roar of approval from the remaining patrons.

Although most incidents lasted only a matter of minutes, if that, there was one occasion, when this was not the case. The setting was in one of those crude and inhospitable Pennsylvania mining towns that had been incorporated on the 1893-94 circuit. The hall in which the Emma Wells Concert Company was to give a performance was situated on the second floor of what can best be described as a rudimentary town hall. Just moments before the opening curtain, a handful of vociferous miners clamoured up the stairs where they were met by R.W. and Tom, engaged in their secondary occupation of selling and collecting tickets. The miners, revelling in their alcoholic euphoria, made it quite clear they were not about to pay admission to a hall which they claimed to have rented for the evening. It soon became apparent that no amount of pacification on the part of the Marks brothers was going to prevent the confrontation that both parties knew was imminent.

Threats and intimidation were no strangers to these showmen who simply delivered an ultimatum – pay the going rate of admission or leave the premises; the latter option would be accomplished by force if necessary. Preferring to drive home their point with actions rather than words, these "hewers of stone" opted to stand and fight. So, with their usual aplomb, R.W. and Tom went to work and, in doing so, gave an admirable account of themselves by routing the would-be gatecrashers and inflicting upon them grievous injuries. Sore and bloodied, the miners, eager to pacify their bruised and battered egos found solace in the contents of a nearby slag heap. After arming themselves with a quantity of rocks, they returned to the hall determined to seek revenge on the thespians.

During the final act of "The Two Orphans," the house suddenly erupted in chaos as a barrage of stones and vindictives invaded the solemnity of the "inner sanctum." Broken glass flew in every direction as frightened spectators dove for cover. The barrage continued throughout the night, pausing only long enough to allow the patrons to go home; but under no circumstances were any cast members allowed to leave. The siege finally came to an end at daybreak when the beleaguered miners cooled their enthusiasm for revenge. One by one they discarded their ammunition and dispersed without any apparent satisfaction, having caused the company nothing more than a slight inconvenience and the loss of a few hours sleep.

Thomas and Margaret (Farrell) Marks, parents of the seven Marks brothers, as shown in an 1895 family photo. *Perth Museum Collection.*

CHAPTER 2

ESTABLISHING ROOTS IN LANARK COUNTY

In order to more fully appreciate the phenomenal success attained by the Marks Brothers, it is necessary to describe in some detail their humble beginnings, commencing with a brief history of their ancestry and rural upbringing in Lanark County.

Prior to the first invasion of the Lanark County forests by Europeans, the area was inhabited by nomadic Indian tribes. The region was noted for the bloody, hostile encounters between the warring *Iroquois du Nord* and the *Iroquois du Sud*. But with the British occupation of the country came a change of affairs. The vast hinterland was thrown open to settlement, and an invading army of immigrants subsequently marched through the verdant woodlands of Upper Canada, armed with the implements of agriculture, having, through necessity, turned their "swords into ploughshares." The United Empire Loyalists from the recently established United States formed the vanguard.

These first pioneers settled along the entire southern frontier of Upper Canada, and their success in establishing a viable existence kindled the zeal of the British government to found other settlements in this, her largest colony. In the year 1815, a proclamation was issued in England, offering free passage and tracts of land to such natives of Britain who might be desirous of proceeding to Canada for the purpose of settling. As a further inducement to potential settlers, this offer was supplemented by free provisions not only during the voyage, but also upon their arrival in the colony and until such time as the land, which was given free to each male immigrant over legal age, could be made to support them. When the first party of settlers arrived in Canada in the autumn of 1815, they found, much to their dismay, that no preparations had been made for their reception by the colonial authorities; thus compelling them to remain in temporary quarters at Brockville until the following summer.

In the fall of 1816, a party of these early settlers, looking toward the early subjugation of the forest, felled a giant elm tree at the site of the present town of Perth. In June of the same year, the "military colony of Perth," which was comprised mainly of British Regulars whose terms of service had expired while in Canada, and who more recently had been members of regiments engaged in the War of 1812, arrived in the vicinity, and were assigned to the surrounding townships of Bathurst and Drummond. Alexander Gourley, the eminent historian who visited the settlement in 1817, gave the following account after noting that nearly one thousand of these soldiers had settled in the area:

> "Some of them are doing well, but many were unpromising settlers, and did indeed only remain until the term of receiving rations expired, or they acquired the right to sell the land given them...At the first settlement of Upper Canada it was not uncommon for soldiers to sell their two hundred acre lots of land for a bottle of rum."[1]

In 1820, the County of Lanark received considerable accessions to her population in the form of the "Lesmahago" and "Transatlantic" Societies of Scottish immigrants, who settled in Dalhousie township; and within a very few years, with the exception of the northern extremities of the county, settlement became quite general.

This pioneer strain was the stock from which the Marks brothers evolved. Although the Marks family has its roots deeply entrenched in Ireland, the name is English in origin, so it is probable the patriarch of the clan was already firmly established in the country when Elizabeth I, ascended to the throne of England. Following the subjugation of Ireland by Oliver Cromwell in 1652, several male members of the Marks family who had fought with Cromwell's "round heads" were rewarded with tracts of land for services rendered.

Robert Marks, the 19th century family patriarch, was born in County Mayo, Ireland, about 1800. Very little is known about this gentleman, other than that he married a woman named Sarah, circa 1824; and while still residing in the "old country" he became the father of at least one child, Matthew. Between the years 1825 and 1832, they emigrated to Canada and raised an additional ten children.

Unfortunately, no documented evidence remains indicating why Robert Marks left the land of his birth to take up residence in the Canadian wilderness. However, it would be safe to assume that a desire to create a better life for his family was the prime motivating factor. The exact date of their arrival in Lanark County also remains a mystery, lost in the annals of history. But there are several references to the surname Marks in the *Bathurst Courier*, a local newspaper of the day, the first mention was in 1836, evidence that the family had resided in the area for some time.

In later years, Ernie, the youngest member of the Marks Brothers theatrical troupe, would record for posterity a brief, yet personal glimpse into the early lives of his grandfather, Robert Marks, and father Thomas Marks. "My father's father," he wrote, "came from Ireland with his wife, but I do not remember him since he was dead at the time I was born. My father grew up where the present farm of Dan Brennan is located." [Concession 5, Lot 2, Bathurst township]

> "It seems that my grandfather in his later life married for the second time. There were two elderly ladies living in a log cabin not far from the homestead and my grandfather married one of these and moved in with them. His family were against it, but grandfather is reported to have said, 'It is a poor rooster that can't scratch for two hens.'
> "This marriage did not work and grandfather came back to live with his son Bob, after three weeks. I understand that the old ladies beat up on him. His son, Bob, carried on in the old homestead and grandfather lived with him until his death."[2]

Robert Marks Sr., according to the personal and agricultural census of 1851-52, was evidently a prosperous farmer, having at that time accumulated 200 acres of land, of which 100 acres were under cultivation. When the next public census was taken in 1861, there was no mention of Robert Marks, leaving one to suspect that he had since left the area or had passed away.

Thomas Marks Sr., father of the celebrated seven brothers, was a second son, born in 1833 on the Bathurst township homestead. Facts surrounding his formative years are sketchy, but we do know he spent the better part of his life tilling the soil and was instrumental in turning Christie Lake into a viable recreation area that had few equals in the Ottawa Valley. The year 1853 held great promise for this resourceful twenty-year- old. It would still be another year before he legally "came of age"; but already he had taken a bride and purchased a farm on the third concession of South Sherbrooke township, which included extensive water frontage on Christie Lake. In conjunction with this initial purchase he acquired another tract of land some three miles distant, on which he cleared one hundred acres and constructed a substantial residence. During the next seventy years the Marks family would acquire well over seven hundred acres of the finest recreational property bordering Christie Lake, and this land would eventually constitute the bulk of the Marks' real estate investments.

Within a few short years, Thomas Marks and family fell victim to the ravages of fire – a scourge which plagued many communities during the early days of settlement. His home, in addition to out-buildings, was consumed in a rampant inferno that originated in a local tannery. Assisted by prevailing winds, it blazed a path of destruction through the width and breadth of South Sherbrooke and surrounding townships, causing extensive damage to both property and livestock. While compiling his brief, but intimate history of the Marks family, Ernie commented on this tragic event:

> "After his marriage he went to live in the 'upper place' where he built a log cabin. It was a very poor location, located in the wilderness and was poor farm land. Some of my brothers were born there. This cabin was burned down in a huge fire that swept the district and when the government representative called the burned-out people to Perth to award them money to start up again, my father declared that all he needed was strength. The government man said that his name would be recorded in Ottawa as the most honest man in Lanark County.
>
> "When he came to Christie Lake after the fire he built another log cabin near where the present Inn (Arliedale) is located, but a few yards to the east. I was not born in this cabin, but in the more imposing house that was later built, but I remember the cabin as a boy and recall that it had a dirt floor and a huge fireplace."[3]

Ernie also recorded the unusual and somewhat poetic circumstances surrounding the chance meeting between his father and the woman who would eventually become his bride, the charming Margaret Farrell:

> "One day he (Thomas) was out with his father when he saw a girl picking her way across a meadow covered with dew. She was picking up her skirts gracefully and father remarked that he was going to make her his wife. That girl turned out to be my mother."[4]

There is no doubt this meeting with the future Mrs. Marks and the conversation carried on between Thomas and the government agent, as reported by Ernie, have about them an air of the dramatic, but considering the very nature of Ernie's chosen profession this is hardly surprising. Yet one cannot discount the possibility that these incidents took place as chronicled.

In those less complicated, but socially structured days of the last century, the sweet and often bittersweet ritual of courting was a family, and more often than not, a public event. In all probability Thomas and Margaret renewed their first fleeting acquaintance at one of the many construction bees that were common at that time in Lanark County. Or perhaps they met and exchanged a few cordial words on the steps or lawn in front of the local church, prior to being formally introduced at an organized picnic or social. Notwithstanding, on November 19, 1853, Thomas Marks and Margaret Farrell became man and wife.

Margaret's parents, Thomas and Eleanor Farrell, came to Perth probably about the same time as Robert Marks Sr., with a contingent of British Army Regulars who had been given tracts of land in the district after completing active service in India. This body of veterans consisted mainly of Scots, Irish, and English "warrior-farmers." According to army tradition of the day the higher the rank, the closer one's land was to the fledgling settlement of Perth. It would appear, however, the Farrells were stationed at the lower end of the chain of command for their land allotment was located some twelve miles west of Perth, near the present village of Maberly.

Tom Farrell originally hailed from Castlebar, County Mayo, Ireland. Both he and his older brother John had seen more than their share of service on the battlefields of India and, although Thomas had decided on starting anew in Canada, John remained in Ireland where he had been deeded the family property. So Thomas, along with several of his brothers made their way to "distant shores," taking with them a considerable amount of money, indicating that, in the "old country," they must have been a family of substance.

Margaret Farrell, born in County Mayo, Ireland, a naturally gifted singer with a flair for fun, had eight brothers and sisters. With the exception of one brother, John Jr., who went to the diamond mines of South Africa, where he made and subsequently lost a fortune, all her family remained in Eastern Ontario, although some moved on to Western Canada in later years. Margaret also had the distinction of being first cousin to Lord Mount Stephen, a pioneer businessman and first president of the Canadian Pacific Railway.

Thomas Marks like many rural inhabitants of his generation, received very little formal education. "My father could not write and mother had to teach him to sign his name," recalled Ernie, "but he was a splendid reader and he read the paper to us without a mistake."[5]

Thomas Marks, born 1833, and Margaret Farrell, parents of the seven Marks brothers, farmed at Christie Lake. Thomas Sr. was revered as a master storyteller and regarded as the strongest man in this part of Lanark County. His wife, Margaret was referred to as a "gifted" Irish lady. Their popularity may have influenced their sons in their choice of theatrical careers. *Perth Museum Collection.*

The elder Marks also had ambitions unrelated to the agricultural profession. It appears he was a man of moderation in all things. "My father's ambition," noted Ernie, "was to be a commander of men or a general in the army. At the various bees he was a leader and organizer. Since he never drank very much he was usually in charge of the responsible jobs like putting on the corners of the barns. He also acted as peace-maker at the fights that arose."[6]

Thomas Marks was held in high esteem by the residents of South Sherbrooke township, so much so, that when he ran for public office in the late 1860s, seeking a term as councillor, he polled the largest majority of votes ever recorded in the municipality. It would be nearly twenty years before he voluntarily relinquished the position. Throughout his life Thomas Marks remained conservative in his political convictions and was guided by his belief in the doctrines expounded by the Church of England.

Existing photographs, posters and playbills of the Marks Brothers depict them as handsome and robust individuals, who, with the exception of Tom and Ernie all sported luxurious handlebar mustaches. R.W. in describing Alex's visage and demeanour paid him the ultimate compliment, "Alex was the living image of Lionel Barrymore."[7]

History and personal recollections record that the brothers inherited their good looks, size, and complexion from their father; who stood well over six feet in height. He is also credited with bestowing upon them more than a liberal amount of his natural histrionic abilities.

Thomas Marks, by all accounts, was an excellent raconteur, and his fame as a storyteller was known throughout the township. On any given Sunday it was the rule, rather than the exception, to have at least a dozen neighbours appear on the doorstep waiting to hear him read aloud the latest edition of the *Weekly Star* or *Family Herald*. During the spring and summer months this attentive audience would sit on the verandah, while Thomas, nestled in a rocking chair, would recount the latest poultry-fattening methods or regale them with the latest fiction and current events. In the winter or inclement weather, the proceedings would move indoors where the congregation would sit at the kitchen table or cluster around the wood stove waiting anxiously to hear the next sentence. "I remember, when I was a youngster," Tom Marks recalled in later years, "seeing as many as thirty horses tied in front of the house on Sunday. People would come from far and near to listen to my father. Most of them stayed all day and, though it never entered my head at the time, I've often wondered since, how we managed to feed them all."[8]

Thomas Marks' rare and unique sense of humour and reading ability resulted in numerous and enthusiastic neighbours camping on his threshold, all ready and willing to take advantage of his fine Irish hospitality. Had he not been as good a farmer as he was a storyteller, it is conceivable that his visitors would have eaten him out of house and home.

An article in the *Perth Courier*, August 2, 1951, refers to Margaret Farrell as "...this great Irish lady [who] brought into their Lanark County home, the soul of Ireland, its music and its laughter, its tenderness and its dreams. The family grew up under that inspiration. They did not have to seek elsewhere for entertainment." Rather, the Marks' home, presided over by Thomas and Margaret, became famous for hospitality and memories of song and family affection. When R.W. was considering his future following the auspicious meeting with King Kennedy in 1876, he undoubtedly knew there was a wealth of unexplained talent under one roof — his family.

Even as grown men, the brothers accorded their father more than ample respect, especially when he was called upon to act as an adjudicator in settling family disputes or arguments; for his word was still law at Christie Lake. As noted earlier Thomas rarely drank alcoholic spirits, but such was not the case with the remaining male family members. Their excessive drinking habits were common knowledge and, in certain instances, well-publized events. Such was probably the case one summer's afternoon when the normally sophisticated and sedate game of croquet suddenly erupted in mayhem. As the game progressed, we are told, tempers flared and voices were raised well above the level allowed within hearing distance of the elder Marks. Raucous behaviour was not, and would not, be tolerated in his presence. But unbeknown to the "combatants," Thomas Sr. was watching the proceedings from the doorway of a nearby woodshed. When it became apparent that matters were deteriorating, he quietly stepped into the fray and, without a single word being uttered, peace was immediately restored.

Thomas Sr. could never afford the luxury of a formal education and he was determined that his offspring should not suffer a similar fate. Thus he insisted they attend the one-room schoolhouse (White's School) that was located a short distance

from the homestead. This institution was "the rock upon which all knowledge was founded" for many rural inhabitants, and such was its contribution to the educational system that only within the last two decades or so did it pass into oblivion. The standard of education in a one-room schoolhouse, was the cornerstone upon which the Marks brothers created an empire.

The Marks family posing for a photograph at the homestead in July 1895.
John Jay had just recently returned from Alaska and Ernie was preparing to enter Perth Collegiate.
From left to right: Alex, Tom, Olivia Mariah (Libby), Thomas Sr., Robert W., Margaret Farrell, Ellen Jane (Nellie), John, Joe, Ernie and McIntyre. *Perth Museum Collection.*

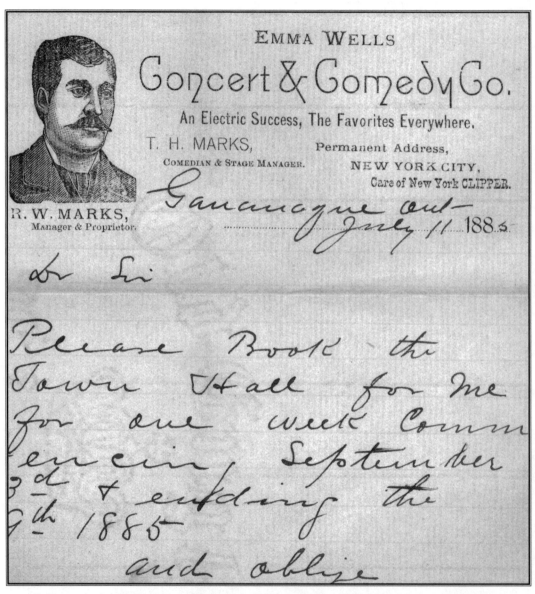

EMMA WELLS

Concert & Comedy Co.

An Electric Success, The Favorites Everywhere.

T. H. MARKS,
COMEDIAN & STAGE MANAGER.

Permanent Address,
NEW YORK CITY,
Care of New York CLIPPER.

R. W. MARKS,
Manager & Proprietor.

Gananoque Ont
July 11 188 5

Dr Sir

Please Book the
Town Hall for Me
for one week Comm
encing September
3d & ending the
9th 1885

and oblige

Following considerable success in the United States, Robert William and his troupe returned to Canada, initially establishing themselves in Renfrew, Ontario. Later, Christie Lake became their headquarters. *Perth Museum Collection.*

CHAPTER 3

CANADA BECKONS – 1882

By 1882, the Emma Wells Concert Company had reached New York City; completing its initial and only trans-continental tour of the United States. At this juncture in their careers R.W., Tom, Emma and Jennie were faced with several important decisions, not the least of which was finding a workable and viable formula that would allow the troupe to break new ground both in the theatrical and territorial sense. A solution to the dilemma was found – Canada beckoned.

The villages, towns and cities of the United States had provided the company with valuable stage exposure and enabled R.W. to hone his business acumen to a fine edge. The tour had provided the troupe with a sizeable nest egg, even though it had been one act in a company of many; for the Emma Wells Concert Company had aligned itself, as was the custom of the day, with a travelling road show under whose "umbrella" upwards of twenty individual artists and troupes had trekked across the countryside. Although this association had proven to be a very profitable one, R.W. had greater goals in mind.

In all probability, the Lanark County showmen had an ulterior motive in wanting to return to the land of their birth: homesickness – that psychological disease peculiar to the human race was no doubt taking its toll. Notwithstanding, common sense dictated that Canada was coming into its own as a "land of theatrical opportunities," as numerous American-based troupes had already discovered. The Dominion, with its wide open spaces and diverse cultures, abounded with opportunities for the Marks Brothers and other enterprising touring companies. In the spring of 1883, the Emma Wells Concert Company found itself headquartered not at Christie Lake or even Perth, but in the Ottawa Valley town of Renfrew. The reason for the troupe using this locale as a base of operation remains unknown. For the next several years the company regularly played the surrounding towns of Pembroke, Arnprior, Almonte, Carleton Place, Smiths Falls and Perth.

The "variety" program was, at this time, being phased out by a more socially acceptable form of entertainment – vaudeville, and it was to this genre that the Emma Wells Concert Company turned its talents. The American theatrical phenomenon, vaudeville, originated in 1883 at Boston, Massachusetts, where a former circus employee, Benjamin Franklin Keith, opened a small museum and show in a vacant candy store next to the old Adams house on Washington Street, called the Gaiety Museum.

Determined to preserve the general plan of the variety show and at the same time give it refinement and even distinction, Keith went after the best available stage talent. He encouraged women and children to patronize his small theatre and began to advertise and describe his show as "vaudeville." He put into operation the idea of continuous performances and was soon able to pay his performers more money that they had been paid in variety, and thus began to command the best talent available. In 1885, Edward F. Albee joined Keith, both of whom would have extensive dealings with R.W. in later years. Together, they organized the Gaiety Opera Company to present, at the lowest popular prices, the new and sensational Gilbert and Sullivan light operas.

When Keith died in 1911, vaudeville was already the most readily attended form of stage entertainment. There were by 1928, approximately one thousand vaudeville theatres entertaining a daily aggregate of two million people by means of well-chosen acts, feature motion pictures and newsreels in every state of the USA and every province of Canada. In 1905, Keith and F.F. Proctor, another vaudeville magnate, joined forces to establish the United Booking Office, which became the official clearing house and engagement bureau for the employment and booking of American vaudeville acts and artists. In 1916, the National Vaudeville Artists Association Incorporated was formed. By 1928, this organization listed about 15,000 artists.[1]

In adopting the vaudeville format as laid out by Keith, which for the most part was in line with his own convictions, R.W. secured the continued success of not only the Emma Wells Concert Company, but also the other Marks Brothers' companies which would one day appear on the horizon.

Within months of relocating to Renfrew, R.W., who was acting as manager and business agent for the four-member partnership, increased his hold on the organization by acquiring the controlling share. Whether the takeover was of design or necessity has little relevance today, but the acquisition gave R.W. a stronger grip on the company and allowed him greater flexibility and freedom in choosing both material and personnel.

With a commanding personality in control, the troupe was able to provide the intelligent citizenry with a varied and consistent array of talent that included dancers, musicians, comedians, acrobats, specialty performers and, of course, melodrama. The availability of orchestras nearly always posed a problem for touring companies in some communities, as proficient musicians were as scarce as a good five-cent cigar. It was, therefore, necessary for troupes to carry their own musicians. R.W. took this one step further and brought along his own piano, a practice he maintained for many years.

R.W.'s shrewd business sense and ability to provide audiences with what they wanted, combined with his professionalism and affability, and with a production format that centred around wholesome, family-orientated entertainment proved to the ticket to fame and fortune for the Emma Wells Concert Company. During the ensuing years this standard of excellence was strictly maintained. Mediocrity found no favour with R.W. It would, in fact, have rung a death knell for the troupe which was now facing stiff competition from the slick and polished American companies that were slipping across the border in ever increasing numbers in search of greener and more lucrative pastures.

Ontario, due in part to its proximity to New York City, the entertainment hub of North America, and coupled with its greater population and growing economic base, was the natural destination for The Nashville Singers, billed as a troupe of coloured entertainers, The Holman Opera Company, the E.T. Goodrich Company and The Tennesseans. The Shaughraun Company, under the management of E.A. McDowell, was also a popular attraction throughout Ontario at this time; in fact, his company had been playing the Perth circuit: Almonte, Carleton Place, Smiths Falls, Arnprior and towns along the St. Lawrence River since 1880. McDowell, it will be remembered, had performed at Winnipeg in 1879, just prior to the arrival of R.W. and King Kennedy.

It is quite likely the Emma Wells Concert Company met with a certain degree of success during the 1883 touring season, but it would seem that the troupe had been largely ignored by local newspapers, as reviews from the time are hard to come by. It was not until October 1884 that a written account of the company's merits appeared in area journals:

> "The Emma Wells Concert Company has been giving a series of their popular entertainments in the Town Hall here [Arnprior] this week under the auspices of the Arnprior Band to well-filled houses. The program given each night is varied and entertaining, consisting of songs, farces and light comedy sketches which afford opportunities for the different members of the company to produce their specialties in a pleasing manner. Miss Emma Wells is an actress of rare merit and in her

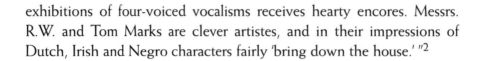

exhibitions of four-voiced vocalisms receives hearty encores. Messrs. R.W. and Tom Marks are clever artistes, and in their impressions of Dutch, Irish and Negro characters fairly 'bring down the house.' "[2]

On October 13, the troupe opened at the Perth Town Hall for a one week engagement. Advertisements placed in the *Perth Courier* proudly proclaimed that the Emma Wells Concert Company's entertainment extravaganza was available to all for the meagre admission of ten cents. A one week's engagement for any touring company amounted to playing Monday through Saturday nights with matinees on Wednesday and Saturday from four o'clock to six o'clock in the afternoon. Matinee prices, however, were reduced slightly, usually in the neighbourhood of five cents.

By now R.W. and his cohorts had acquired a dedicated following in rural Eastern Ontario and the northeastern United States; the latter having been won over on their frequent jaunts across the border when lapses in Canadian bookings permitted. R.W. and Tom had taken the attitude with regard to theatrical territory that the border between Canada and the United States was purely imaginary. During the next forty years the Marks brothers and their companies proceeded to "invade" the southern republic at will, confident that their reception would equal if not surpass the last time they performed there, and indeed, such was the case. They felt and deservedly so, their companies could offer American audiences better amusement than ever came from New York City; and their old box office receipts indicate that many thousands of Americans must have thought so, too.[3]

By 1885, the Emma Wells Concert Company had become deeply entrenched in the entertainment psyche of rural Eastern Ontario. Townspeople, by contrast with city dwellers, retained and cultivated Victorian standards and ideals. Invariably, entertainment and other social activities took place at home, with the whole family taking part; but when organized entertainments in surrounding towns and villages proved to a viable alternative, the companies merely became an extension of the home life. Whenever a play was presented by the local dramatic club or itinerant touring company, the whole family attended. It was, of course, paramount that the dramas presented were morally correct and typified the Victorian ideals of the day; and those companies, including the Emma Wells Concert Company and later the Marks Brothers' troupes, who practised this philosophy soon gained favour for their moral reliability.

The following extract taken from an 1894 newspaper clipping outlines R.W.'s stand on the subject of moral entertainment:

"It is gratifying to know that you have put on elevating, clean and decent dramas," remarked the reporter as he addressed R.W.

"You will never find anything else with us," he replied. "We do not cater to the class which requires coarse jest, questionable allusion, anything but what is pure and elevating. Should it ever be necessary for us to do that we will quit the business. But we do not think we shall have any trouble on that account. We have never uttered one word that would offend the most fastidious and refined."[4]

During the 1880s and 1890s touring companies offered their audiences a myriad of entertainment styles ranging from bawdy variety shows, burlesque, melodrama, and performances which catered solely to Victorian ideals and sensibilities. Patrons who flocked in droves to the local opera house or music hall could see the likes of W. H. Harris Great Nickle Plate Shows, The Norman Comedy Company, B. Mendelson's New York Opera Company, The McDowell Troupe, and for those who preferred a more sedate from of entertainment, the John B. Doris' New Monster Moral Show.

It should be remembered that to a farmer or small town dweller in Canada before the turn of the century, melodrama was, in a sense, realism. It dealt with life as he understood it and problems he feared, such as an erring daughter. The daughter who compromised her virtue was a disgrace to the family, and the outraged parents' typical reaction was to disown her with banishment from the homestead. Of course, an explanation would be offered to show that the daughter's indiscretions were really not as bad as they seemed. Afterwards, life would become tolerable again and all was forgiven.

Patrons of the popular theatre, for the most part, demanded any stage offering should end happily. Life as they saw it was a continual struggle for survival, and few relished the idea of sitting through a production that only reinforced their greatest fears – that life in general offered only heartache and deprivation. So, as the curtain unfolded, the worries of the outside world were all but forgotten for two hours as they immersed themselves in the comings and goings of the evening's fare.

Villains were villains, dressed in black riding boots, black sombreros, white buckskin trousers, and cut-away Prince Albert coats. They sported rapier thin handlebar mustaches which required the occasional twist (strictly for effect) as they leered lecherously at the virginal heroines who were spurning their unwarranted advances. And, of course, heroes were heroes, with their wavy blonde hair and white shirts open at the neck, well-worn riding breeches and brown riding boots. It was not hard to discern who was good and who was evil: the costumes said it all. The heroine wore calico gowns while the siren was resplendent in her satins and velvets. The heroine bounced across the stage while the villainess slinked her way to infamy.

Whenever the hero or heroine spurned temptation it was with the full hearted endorsement of the audience. Their actions were intended to plant a moral lesson in youthful hearts. But youthful hearts were inclined to envy the villain and the vamp who never seemed to suffer half as many buffets from fate as the more admirable characters. "Virtue in rags" never failed to make women cry (in the theatre) and the click of the duellists' swords motivated many young men to spend their next strike pay on fencing lessons.

Productions such as "Why Girls Leave Home," "All For Love," "Brother Against Brother," "The Girl And The Bandit" and "Within The Law," portrayed life as many would have it. Some of the aforementioned titles may or may not have been included in the repertoire of the Emma Wells Concert Company during the 1880s, but in later years they would become standard productions for the Marks Brothers' companies.

"Within The Law," written by American playwright, Bayard Veiller, was a favourite Marks Brothers production. The play amounted to a vigorous arraignment of the American legal system — attacking the iniquities of police methods and the system of punishment. The play also seethes with revolt against social conditions of the day which make these and other injustices possible.

The heroine, Mary Turner, is a shop girl employed in a department store at six dollars a week. She is accused unjustly of a theft and, despite her innocence, the attorney for her employer, Edward Gilder, is able to secure a conviction. The question of guilt or innocence is a minor matter with the store owner. He needs to make an example and does it. Before going to prison, the girl has the opportunity to deliver a ringing tirade against department store life – the long hours and low wages furnishing the conditions on which, in her mind, white slavery thrives.

By the end of her term, the heroine has conceived a fanatical idea of avenging herself on both the employer and the system that have been responsible for her downfall. She gathers about her a little band of former crooks and convicts, teaches them to make money dishonestly – without technical violations of the law, however, – and is soon in possession of the power that capital brings. To wipe out the personal grudge against her employer, she lures his son into a clandestine marriage with her.

In order to break up the gang, against whose operations they have hitherto been powerless, the police finally resort to a trap to catch one of its members in an overt violation of the law. A "stool pigeon" is employed to tempt him into robbing Gilder's house. Mary happens to be in her father-in-law's house with her husband at the time set for springing the trap. When the gangster discovers that his supposed pal is a police informer, he shoots him dead and hands the smoking gun to Mary's husband. When the police arrive and find the dead body on the floor, Mary explains that her husband has shot him. As the dead intruder was a burglar, the killing is "within the law."

The last act furnishes proof of Mary's innocence of the original crime, and she is free to commence life on a new basis with a husband she has grown to love.

In those unsophisticated days, the corn was also very green. Actors and comics laid the audience in the aisles with such gems as: "I sent my wife to the Thousand Islands for a vacation...a week on each island." "Are oysters healthy? I never heard one complain." ... "You can drive a horse to drink but a pencil must be lead."

As the tide of immigration increased on both sides of the border during the 1880s, ethnic jokes became the vogue. The stage of that era quickly mirrored the lives of its audience. As the first Irish, German, Italian and Jewish immigrants disembarked at the ports of Halifax and Quebec, each nationality was shown its stereotype on stage; usually portrayed at the level of the lowest common denominator. Thus, Irish characters wore ear to ear chin whiskers, called "sluggers" or "gallaways." The players invariably carried a walking stick, drank whiskey from a hip flask, jigged and never spoke without saying "begorra." Germans were portrayed as having over-sized shoes, fancy vests with heavy watchchains, and accents that murdered the English language.

But attitudes changed during those years of prosperity just after the turn of the century, when minorities achieved a new economic and social dignity. They no longer chose to laugh at the derision. Gradually, the gaudy Irishman, Jew, German and Italian, gave way to the "neat" comic. Unlike the less flattering portrayals of past years, actors and comics were well-dressed and attractive. They relied primarily on wit and talent for laughter and applause, but were always careful to retain a bit of the old brogue or dialect; making themselves more popular than they had ever been while performing slapstick routines.

In late August 1885, the Emma Wells Comedy Company (it is not known why R.W. substituted comedy for concert) opened the 1885-86 season in the Eastern Ontario town of Listowel, and again the company was the recipient of several printed accolades; but such was not the case with other companies who had performed in the community:

> "On Thursday night last week the Emma Wells Comedy Company began a series of entertainments which concluded Wednesday evening this week. As a rule the entertainments given in this place by travelling troupes have not been of the most popular character — as a result, the public have become largely indifferent to any announcement which they may make."

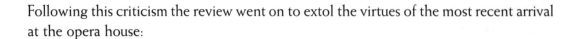

Following this criticism the review went on to extol the virtues of the most recent arrival at the opera house:

> "At the first entertainment last week, the audience was anything but a large one, but those who were present soon discovered that something out of the ordinary line was being presented. The impersonation by Mr. T. H. Marks, of Irish and Negro characters were really first class and his stump speeches fairly brought down the house. Mr. R.W. Marks also sustained his parts well in addition to acting as general manager of the entertainment. Miss Jennie Ray gave some excellent solos, and in several plays sustained her character with good taste and judgment. But the star of the company is Miss Emma Wells, and her performance alone as a vocalist or at the piano, would make a really first class entertainment in themselves.
>
> "On the second night and during each succeeding night of the entertainment the house was crowded and so much that on Monday and Tuesday nights every available space was occupied, and a large number could not gain admission for want of room. We only express the opinion of the public in saying that the Emma Wells Company, has given the most popular and in many respects the best entertainments ever given in this place and should they return at any future time to pay us another visit, the reputation they made will not be forgotten."[5]

The following year, 1886, saw the company once again touring the northern United States, and in particular, New York State, which would remain one of the Marks Brothers' favourite playdates. Here, their popularity seldom waned, not even in those years when melodrama and vaudeville were supplanted by motion pictures, radio, and a general return to legitimate theatre. The same year witnessed another influx of American-based companies crossing the border into Canada; this migration was due in part to the completion of the Canadian Pacific Railway in 1885. Ontario, it would seem, had much to offer Jimmie Fax, King of Komics, Harrigan's Hibernian Company, Hamlin's Wizard Oil Concert and Advertising Company, (one of the first new-breed medicine shows to play in the region) and Lester and Allen's Minstrels, whose main attraction was John L. Sullivan, the eminent bare-knuckled boxing champion.

It would also appear that 1886 was the first year in which R.W., along with selected members of the company, began returning to Christie Lake for extended periods during the off-season. This annual ritual would continue until the 1920s when the last of the Marks Brothers' companies bowed before the final curtain. With the exception of John,

who remained in British Columbia, and Ernie, who eventually became Mayor of Oshawa, when the brothers left the road they spent their remaining years basking in the cool breezes of the lake.

The July 8, 1886, edition of the *Perth Courier* noted the return of R.W. and Tom to Christie Lake:

> "The Marks brothers of the Emma Wells Comedy Company arrived home to their father Mr. Thomas Marks, Christie Lake, on July 5th. The company has been on the road 41 weeks this season in Ontario and New York State; they open next season September 6th, at Ogdensburg, New York. This has been the best playing season since 1881. Miss Wells, the star, and Miss Ray, the soubrette are going to Kansas to visit friends for six weeks, but they will rejoin the company at Mr. Marks' during the latter part of August."

Even during the off-season R.W. and Tom seldom missed the opportunity to entertain in the surrounding villages and towns. Neither did they hesitate to accept an invitation to perform at church socials or their fund raising events. In later years it was not uncommon for each the Marks brothers' companies to play at least one benefit concert at St. Stephen's Anglican Church, in Bathurst township, the source of religious instruction for the Marks' family.

There is no indication that R.W. and Tom, or for that matter, any of the brothers held strong religious convictions or were even regular church-goers. But they did realize that the church-going segment of society now constituted the lion's share of their audience; yet there remained many individuals in the religious rank and file, who, for obvious reasons, shunned the notion of attending theatricals. It was this faction that R.W. conspired to attract with an innovative plan of action. Each Sunday, whenever possible, the troupe, dressed in its finery would parade through the community in which it was playing and make its way to church. However, there were certain drawbacks to this publicity ploy – depending on the number of different denominations in the town it was not uncommon for company members to attend three different services. This weekly ritual had the desired effect, demonstrating that the Marks Brothers' companies not only presented entertainments that were "clean in theme and treatment," but the players were also God-fearing individuals who embodied the very essence of their wholesome productions.

In keeping with their mandate of playing church functions, Tom and Jennie Ray performed at a picnic in Maberly, on July 6, 1886, under the auspices of St. Stephen's

Church. Tom was the hit of the show and received excellent reviews for his character recitations and vocal renditions of a "New Church Again" and "Miss Julia O'Toole."

During the latter part of July, the entire company played a number of smaller communities throughout the district, including Westport, Newboro and the Village of Lanark, before giving a farewell picnic at the lake. In years to come these picnics, held prior to the season opener, would become a regular feature at Christie Lake, and were used primarily for presenting new plays and features in a relaxed atmosphere before a paying audience.

Prior to the start of the new 1886-87 season, which was scheduled to open at Alexandria Bay, New York, on September 4, (the location and date had been changed from the original opening date of September 6, at Ogdensburg, New York) R.W. acquired several supporting acts comprised mainly of singers and dancers; but an old trouper had also been added to the payroll – King Kennedy. At this time Kennedy had dropped the "Mysterious Hindu from the Bay of Bengal" appellation and was billed simply as a ventriloquist.

When Emma Wells returned from Kansas on August 7, 1886, (Jennie never made the trip) she went directly to Christie Lake and soon after her arrival purchased a waterfront property from Thomas Marks Sr. She paid one hundred dollars for the lot and, naming it "Red Cedar Wild", immediately commissioned the building of a summer residence.

Little is known of the Emma Wells Comedy Company's whereabouts or activities during the first ten months of the 1886-87 season, but in mid-June 1887, following an appearance in Carleton Place, the local newspaper reported the troupe, at least in the reporter's eyes, had acquired a greater degree of professionalism and refinement since its last appearance the previous year. On opening night Carleton Place residents cheered, jeered, booed and hissed their way through a performance of "All On The Quiet," and then, in typical fashion, R.W. left them laughing with the comical farce "Our Lodgers."

The review also made mention of Alex Marks and, although little is said about his acting abilities, there is no doubt he conducted himself credibly. Alex, however, never felt comfortable in front of the footlights and chose instead to forsake his budding acting career for the less demanding role of advance agent. In this capacity he would travel ahead of the troupe, usually by several weeks, in order to secure concert halls and accommodations. The advance agent was also responsible for arranging the company's transportation needs and providing newspaper editors with recent reviews. Another facet of this position entailed the hiring of youngsters, for a few cents per day, to post advertising handbills throughout the town.

Home Rule at Last.

A GRAND PIC-NIC

Under the auspices of the Renowned

EMMA WELLS Comedy Company

WILL BE HELD AT

Mr. Thomas Marks' Grove

CHRISTIE'S LAKE, Lanark County, on

SATURDAY AUG. 21.

The Lake is one of the pleasantest resorts in the country, and under such management the Pic-Nic will certainly be a success.

AMUSEMENTS.

A large Platform will be erected for dancing during the day and evening. An Orchestra will furnish excellent music, consisting of first and second Violin, Cornet and the splendid Piano of the Emma Wells Co. Under canvas in the evening the EMMA WELLS COMEDY CO. will give one of their Unparalleled Performances, assisted by the Renowned Ventriloquist, King Kennedy. Swings Boats, Croquet, etc., will be furnished for lovers of such amusements.

SPORTS

PROF. L. J. DeHAVEN, from Rochester, N. Y., will make a GRAND BALLOON ASCENSION at one o'clock p m. Also a Base Ball Match between picked nines from Perth and the Lake for a Silver Cup. A Punt and Tub Race on the bay, open to all.

REFRESHMENTS.

Excellent Meals will be furnished on the grounds at any time during the day or evening. The stands will have the various drinks for sale. Fruits, Ice Cream &c. Hay and oats and stabling can be had for the horses. A cordial invitation is extended to all. For further particulars see programmes or apply to

R. W. MARKS.
Manager.

July 20th, 1886.

A poster advertising a "Grand Picnic" featuring the Emma Wells Comedy Company to be held at Christie Lake, released to the public on July 20, 1886. Obviously, King Kennedy is still with the troupe. The headline "Home Rule At Last" likely refers to the movement advocating devolved government for Ireland, indicating the Irish origins of the Marks family. *Perth Museum Collection.*

Although it is not known how much R.W. paid to rent a hall or theatre in the 1880s, we do know, however, that in 1905, the rental fee for the common room in the Perth Town Hall was fourteen dollars a day for theatrical productions, with a twenty percent discount during the summer months.

By early September 1887, the company had fulfilled its theatrical commitments in Eastern Ontario and preparations began in earnest for an extended tour of what would be new and "uncharted" territory – the states of Vermont, Massachusetts, New Hampshire and Connecticut. It was a gruelling and arduous circuit initially, an endless stream of one-night stands, the actors playing to half-filled houses and to less-than-enthusiastic audiences. Gradually their lot improved and as the company's reputation grew so did the gate receipts. When the season closed in June 1889, R.W., Tom, and other company members returned once again to the relative comfort of Christie Lake.

This yearly retreat to the lake served a twofold purpose. Firstly, it offered R.W., Tom, and company members a well-earned respite from the rigorous touring schedule. Secondly, it provided the brothers with additional income insomuch as contract players were required to pay for their lodgings while rehearsing new plays and features for the forthcoming season. Although this practice might be considered unethical by today's standards, it should be noted that both R.W. and Tom had commissioned the building of numerous cottages on the lake which afforded performers a certain amount of luxury and the privilege of reposing by a lake that had few equals in Eastern Ontario. In order accommodate this influx of performers, R.W. had built a rehearsal hall which sat on the crest of a hill, affording an unsurpassed view of the lake. Unfortunately, no physical evidence of this structure remains today, but from all accounts it was a building of some magnitude. Here, R.W. and Tom mapped out routes and selected plays which would be used during the season, while actors, musicians, dancers, and comedians perfected their routines; other company members, assisted by local residents, created and painted the elaborate scenery.

For the next three years the Emma Wells Comedy Company continued touring the Ontario and New York State circuit, which had now been expanded to include the communities of Lindsay, Peterborough, Orillia, Cobourg, Barrie and Newcastle.

Leisure time at Christie Lake was always welcome. That may be R.W. standing front left, partly obscured by a tree. From 1886 on, the theatrical group would return to the lake over the summer, to prepare for the next season and to relax with the Marks family. *Perth Museum Collection.*

Thomas (Tom) Henry Marks possessed a strong sense of showmanship and was much aware of the value of publicity. It was Tom, of all the brothers, who developed his gift for comedy into popular acts that enthralled his audiences. *Perth Museum Collection.*

CHAPTER 4

TOM MARKS – A KEEN EYE FOR BUSINESS AND A FLAIR FOR COMEDY

At the age of nineteen, Tom Marks had begun to seriously evaluate his future. A life spent hoeing potatoes and pulling weeds held little appeal for this ambitious Lanark County farm boy; but at this stage in his life Tom was not certain of the direction his ambitions should be channelled.

The nineteenth century was an era when young men of limited means were not required to give overdue consideration to acquiring a skilled vocation, but tradition required that each man discover what fate had in store, and should all else fail, at least be content with his situation in life, whether he be a field hand or store clerk. After many hours of deliberation, Tom came to the conclusion there were better things in store for him than remaining on the farm, and he was determined to enjoy them.

In the spring of 1876, according to James A. Cowan,[1] word circulated around Christie Lake that the annual state fair in far-off Minneapolis, was not to be missed. The uncompromising sense of adventure that had spurred Tom's forefather to leave his ancestral home for the broad expanse of Canada, now burned deep within him; and with it came the realization that the Minneapolis State Fair might, indeed, offer opportunities peculiar to his unique personality and talents.

> But leaving the shores of Christie Lake in those days was no easy task
> for a young man of Tom's limited financial means. However, he soon
> found a benefactor, (perhaps his father) who loaned him enough money
> to purchase a train ticket with a little to spare. According to Cowan, the
> state fair offered few rewards for this intrepid traveller, and when the

gala concluded, Tom moved on. Just as he was running out of money, he found himself in an impoverished Minnesota town. Realizing the futility of his situation, he calculated with some degree of apprehension the length of time it would take to walk from this over-rated hovel back to Ontario. He came to the conclusion that walking was impossible, even for a young man of his physical stature and determination. As luck would have it, Tom made the acquaintance of a gentleman who loaned him one hundred dollars. In those days a hundred dollars constituted a king's ransom, and this outpouring of generosity from a virtual stranger was indicative of Tom's dynamic and magnetic personality. Leaving his trunk and other personal effects as a token of his good faith, Tom, for reasons known only to him, stepped down from the train (on a damp and dreary night) at Eau Claire, Wisconsin.

"Never in all my life," he declared, "have I been as ill as I was on that night and what is more, with one of the worst diseases in the world, barring love. I was suffering from home-sickness. I could smell the wind off the lake and see the lights shining on the water in front of the farm house, I was tempted. I wanted to take that hundred dollars, forget about repaying it and buy a one-way ticket home. I'll never know why I didn't."[2]

After taking one last look at the departing train, Tom left the station and trudged wearily through the rain-slicked streets searching for suitable lodgings. Following a good night's sleep, his spirit revived, but craving further rest and relaxation he decided that a day at the races would fit the bill. Tom's habit of indulging whole-heartedly in "life's little pleasures" led him to wager all that remained of his capital. But, as luck would have it, he walked away, more specifically, rode away from the racetrack with no less than eighteen hundred dollars bulging from his pockets.

The races concluded, Tom decided to leave the track in grand style, and did so by hiring the finest carriage available. The hiring of this swank conveyance served a dual purpose, for during the afternoon he had met the governor's daughter and had obtained permission to escort her home. Not only did the carriage serve the purpose for which it was originally intended, but also pointed out to the elite of Eau Claire, that this Lanark County farm boy was as gallant a squire as any Wisconsin youngblood. When Tom bid farewell to the young woman, he never expected to see her again. He never did.

It wasn't until forty years later, noted Cowan, that Tom, accompanied by his daughter, Arlie, stopped at that same Minnesota town where he had found himself penniless and yet had managed to secure financial assistance, that he remembered his trunk:

> "Quick," he said, as the train started to pull away from the station, "we've got to get off here, I've forgotten something."
>
> "What?" asked a surprised Arlie.
>
> "A trunk," came Tom's reply. "I left it here forty years ago and I've never thought of it since until this minute."[3]

Little is known about Tom's exploits during the next several years, but Cowan reported he found employment as a government reporter under President James Abram Garfield; but collaborative information supporting this contention is doubtful. Cowan recorded that Tom joined Garfield's expedition on the Yellowstone Survey, which was conducted between Chamberlain, South Dakota and the Little Missouri River. Tom supposedly remained in this capacity for two years before meeting Buffalo Bill Cody, who was then playing legitimate theatre. However, it is highly unlikely that Tom met the famed Westerner at this time, as Cody's last stage appearance was in 1874, when he performed in "The Scouts of the Plains," at Buffalo, New York; whereas, Tom, according to Cowan, didn't leave Ontario for Minneapolis until 1876.

Notwithstanding, the story is entertaining enough and deserves repeating. Cody, after leaving the army, embarked on a theatrical career and, in 1873, formed the Buffalo Bill Combination, featuring himself, a number of Indians, cowboys and a variety of actors performing western melodramas. In 1883, Cody changed both the format and the name of his company to Buffalo Bill's Wild West. Cody, it is said, took an immediate liking to the young Canadian and offered him a position as advance agent for the Combination. It was not long before Tom was given a small part in a new play the company was rehearsing. On opening night Tom proved to be a hit; as a result, Buffalo Bill intimated that the young man should forsake the position of advance agent and engage himself in the creative side of show business.

An in-depth search of records by curator, Paul Fees, at the Buffalo Bill Historical Center in Cody, Wyoming, has failed to uncover any information that would link Tom and Cody, either in a business or personal sense. But Mr. Fees has made an interesting observation:

> "We have been unable to find any reference to Thomas Marks in connection with either the Buffalo Bill Combination or Buffalo Bill's Wild West. The connection is not unlikely. Cody had many friends and

relatives in Ontario and spent a great deal of time in Eastern Ontario, particularly after the turn of the century. His cousin and business partner John Frank Cody, was from London."[4]

Tom, according to Cowan, remained with Cody for sometime before striking out with a black-faced minstrel show, in which, by all accounts, he perfected the Irish brogue and Negro dialect that would one day become his stock and trade.

At this point in Tom's career, we can only speculate as to his whereabouts; but one might surmise he continued performing with minstrel shows before eventually returning to Canada. His reasons for coming back to the land of his birth will no doubt remain a mystery as Tom never once indicated in any of his numerous interviews why he left the United States at this stage in his career. Maybe it was a touch of homesickness, or perhaps he had heard that R.W. was now making a name for himself and decided that a union of their respective talents would benefit both. It is irrelevant today as to why he returned to Canada, but stories written about R.W. and Tom, whether fact or fiction, add greatly to the mystique of these gentlemen.

Tom, like his brother, knew the importance of keeping oneself in the public eye, and this was accomplished in part by window dressing his off-stage and out-of-door appearances. Plug hats, patent leather shoes that shone like mirrors, Prince Albert coats, silk shirts and broad cravats, complemented by ever-present diamonds, ensured the Marks Brothers' notoriety. The diamonds, which, during their early theatrical careers were merely cut-glass, grew both in size and abundance according to their bank balances. These "baubles," in the form of rings or stickpins, were constant companions and seldom were off their person. Audiences were often amazed to see, on the stage, a tramp, pauper, or policeman, wearing jewellery that the crown heads of Europe would envy. These diamonds were almost as famous as the Marks Brothers themselves.

Gimmicks were a necessary evil for the early itinerant showman, and the brothers, especially Tom, were masters at the game. By 1894, he had his own theatrical company and, like R.W., was active across Ontario and the northern American states. Whenever he came to town, Tom made it a point to hire a flashy rig for personal transportation. Accompanying Tom as he made his appointed rounds, visiting his many friends and acquaintances, was Buster. Buster was Tom's pet bulldog – an animal possessed of rare talent. Buster provided the sort of entertainment that kept spectators coming back for more and gave Tom the kind of publicity which eventually turned fanfare into dollars. Buster, it seemed, competed very successfully with Tom's diamonds for public attention. One of the canine's favourite tricks entailed driving the rig, securing the reins in his teeth. He followed this antic by holding the tether while Tom went visiting.

Well into the twentieth century the Canadian West was still "rough and ready," and like its American counterpart, contained more than its share of incorrigibles. But the fledgling city of Calgary offered some respite for Tom and his company from the antics of overzealous cowboys and townspeople in the more remote areas. The affable Easterner, on a previous visit, so we are told by Cowan, had made the acquaintance of an English aristocrat-rancher named, Beresford. This Beresford, according to Tom, was a man of great mystery and although professing a noble ancestry, little was known of him. But he was, and remained so until his death, Tom's intimate friend. Beresford, accompanied by all his ranch hands, including the foreman, who was a great believer in maintaining order, appeared at every performance.

"When he [foreman] was in the house," Tom said, "there never was a peep from any unruly visitor."[5]

The foreman, being large in stature, gave the impression he would sooner split a man in half than have one of Tom's productions rudely interrupted. "Beresford himself was an unusual type even for the west," Tom remarked a few years before his death. "For an Englishman, he was the nearest thing to an American westerner I have ever run across. He had a drooping British mustache, but he talked with a half-Yankee drawl. He always chewed tobacco. I think he must have chewed it in his sleep." Tom continued:

> "The people of the west always were reasonable folks. I never thought the west should be rated as hard territory to play. A show was always given a chance to make good. If it did, it had only scattered bits of trouble. If performances were poor or if a manager tried to put something over on the public, he nearly always got was coming to him – but that is a different matter altogether."[6]

When Western Canada finally came into its own, those years when real estate was a prime commodity and oil was supplanting gold, Tom was right there – holding both land deeds and oil stock. In fact, he developed a veritable passion for real estate transactions. But his investments were not restricted to these commodities alone; he also acquired extensive mining interests in British Columbia, thanks, no doubt, to his brother, John, who had left Christie Lake for find his fortune in the gold fields of the Klondike and British Columbia. However, during the Calgary hysteria of 1911, Tom made his largest investments in the oil market. He was luckier than most in this respect, as he emerged from the frenzy relatively unscathed and considerably richer than most of his counterparts.

His first venture into oil speculation began when a fleeting acquaintance offered to sell him five hundred shares of stock in the "Dingman Well," for one dollar a share. This gentleman had previously purchased the shares for five times that amount, but having fallen on hard times he found it necessary to sell his stock in order to keep his creditors at bay. When "all hell broke loose" and the well spewed forth its "black gold" with unheard-of regularity, Tom immediately assigned another member of the company to take charge of coming engagements and hurried to Calgary. "I sold my stock as soon as I got in," he recounted. "I rated myself as a smart financier since I got twenty-nine dollars a share for it. Then I decided to stay a day or so longer and speculate with the money I had made on the first deal. But on the night of my arrival I developed the world's worst toothache. My face swelled out of shape; the pain was terrible and I didn't as much as go out on the street, much less buy stocks." Perhaps that was fortunate:

> "The next day my condition was not improved when I heard a rumour that the shares I had sold for twenty nine dollars were then worth ninety eight dollars each. As soon as I was better, I had to rush back to my company and I never got a chance to risk another nickel before the boom went to pieces. That is possibly the reason I made the money I did."[7]

Tom's adventures in the west form the basis of may stories and anecdotes; some are based on fact, while others stem more from a vivid imagination than anything else. During his extensive career there were occasions when Tom's ready Irish wit and quick thinking saved both his reputation and those of his players, especially when they found themselves in situations that could have severely compromised the very existence and credibility of all the Marks Brothers' companies. The following but unsubstantiated story depicts one such incident attributed to the sharp-witted Tom Marks, who along with his troupe were entertaining the residents of a small prairie town when they came to the attention of a local clergyman seated "front and centre." Accompanying Tom on this western swing was an actor named John Kane, who is reported to have been a native of Perth. Kane was playing the leading role in "The Parish Priest," and from all accounts, had perfected his character and mastered the necessary histrionics to ensure his success in the part. In reality, however, nature had not bestowed upon Kane the virtues needed to obtain the social stature that would qualify him for the priesthood. But the clergyman believed otherwise, and was so impressed with Kane and his feigned holiness, that he made his way to the hotel where the company was staying in the hopes of professing his admiration for the young man.

Tom, fortunately, greeted the clergyman in the lobby and was grateful to hear of the latter's intentions. At that moment, much to Tom's chagrin, Kane, who was now

A later photograph of Tom Marks with his wife Ella (left) and daughter Arlie. The bull terrier, Buster, held the reins of Tom's horse as a way of attracting a crowd. *Perth Museum Collection.*

feeling the effects of a three-hour drought, proceeded unsteadily down the stairs, dressed only in undershirt and trousers, clutching in one hand a large pitcher of beer.[8]

"Why there's the priest," exclaimed the cleric, as he started towards the swaggering Kane.

"I would not disturb him now," Tom remarked hastily. "You see he's taking his daily exercise; running up and down the stairs. This is the third time, so you won't see him for a while."

"But he's carrying a pitcher of beer," cried the startled clergyman.

"Always does it," remarked Tom. "Something to do with balance."[9]

This is another beer-soddened incident, not necessarily attributed to Tom or any

of the other Marks' companies, but which demonstrates the potential hazards of performing the temperance drama, "Ten Nights in a Barroom," once too often. Ordinarily the heavy drinking scenes in this production were faked, empty bottles or coloured water were used to simulate whiskey and beer. But on one occasion a group of admirers substituted the empty bottles with several cases of the real thing, much to the surprise of the performers. As the scene progressed with increasing zeal, one actor after another slammed his beer mug on the bar and ignoring his lines, barked, "Set 'em up again, boy! C'mon fellas, this one is on me!" As circumstance would have it, the well-rehearsed script fell by the wayside. It is doubtful that any of the lines were heard at all over the continuous gurgling. The curtain was eventually brought down on a scene of "unrehearsed" realism, to the great delight of the players.[10]

The four dashing showmen, Tom, Alex, Joe and R.W,. in an 1891 publicity photograph.
Perth Museum Collection.

Before coming to Canada, May Adelaide Bell was already an established stage beauty in her native New York City. Among other performers of note, she had worked with the famous Canadian comedienne Marie Dressler. *Perth Museum Collection.*

CHAPTER 5

EXIT EMMA – ENTER MAY A. BELL

By the early 1890s, touring companies were still facing hostile situations in most Canadian and American communities whose population largely consisted of miners, shantymen, lumberjacks and others who enjoyed more than the occasional raucous night on the town. One might expect that these rough and tumble days were a thing of the past, but such was not the case. As noted in an earlier chapter, R.W. and Tom expended a great deal of time and energy rousting undesirables who relished the idea of disrupting a performance for the sheer pleasure of it.

It was now generally accepted, that once the Marks Brothers had played a town and cleaned it up, so to speak, other troupes which had formerly stayed away would follow in droves. In fact, when the word went out that R.W. and Tom were coming into an area, the leading citizens of some communities would often band together and offer them special inducements to play an engagement.

Such was the case in 1892, when the two were scouting the town of Dundas, Ontario, for inclusion on their circuit. Prior to their arrival, Joe Murphy, a famous Irish actor of the day, had just been run out of town much to the horror of the townspeople. A deputation of Dundas residents and businessmen offered R.W. and Tom free use of the town hall for an indefinite period if they would consent to bring their show to town. They agreed. On opening night R.W. glanced through the house and noticed there was not one single woman in the audience. There was, however, a dramatic and hostile atmosphere in the building, one which did not emanate from the stage. Even before the performance commenced several spectators were ejected or refused admission. The attitude of these two showmen was so belligerent indeed, that no outbreak occurred, though there was some indication that trouble was coming when the house began to fill; but the show went on without a hitch.

The town of Dundas was most appreciative and the remainder of the company's stay was equally peaceful. Financially, the engagement was one of the most successful in the long history of the Marks Brothers undertakings.

Life on the road and at Christie Lake in 1893, was not as idyllic as it might seem on the surface; for all was not well between R.W. and Emma Wells. The same could be said for the all-but-forgotten romance between Tom and Jennie Ray. We can only speculate on the cause of what might best be described as R.W.'s "pending divorce," but in all likelihood it stemmed from disenchantment with his mistress of eleven years. In the meantime, it was business as usual and the company remained intact, playing its appointed circuit.

The 1893-93 touring season closed on June 6, 1893, when the Marks Brothers returned to Christie Lake. Shortly thereafter, the *Perth Courier* announced that R.W. and Tom had indeed returned home, but the newspaper failed to give even the slightest hint as to the whereabouts of Misses Emma Wells and Jennie Ray, other than to say that flags were flying over their residence.

Less than a month after returning to the lake, the company was playing a number of smaller communities in Lanark and surrounding counties. Starting in early June and ending on October 23, the Marks Brothers' Comedy Company (Emma Wells' name had now been dropped from the company title) played McDonald's Corners, Almonte, Pembroke, Perth and the Village of Lanark. In Lanark the three-act comedy farce "McGinty's Troubles" was performed. The Town of Perth was graced with three performances during this period on three separate dates. This schedule in itself was not unusual as Perth was often used by the Marks brothers as a testing ground for their new and revamped productions.

The summer of 1893 marked a milestone in R.W.'s theatrical career and established him as a manager/producer on an international scale, for he now began importing American actors as contract players. Until then, whenever additional actors, musicians or variety players were required to augment the company, usually for one or two nights, R.W. and Tom hired local artists in each town. However, The Field's Mandolin Company of Boston and Alexander B. Butler of Chicago, were the first of many American acts that would join the Marks Brothers' companies in the years ahead.

Rave reviews were now a common occurrence for this company and when it played the Almonte Opera House in September, the troupe, on opening night, was greeted by the applause of five hundred souls. The *Almonte Times* of September 26, 1893, gave a glowing account of the performance:

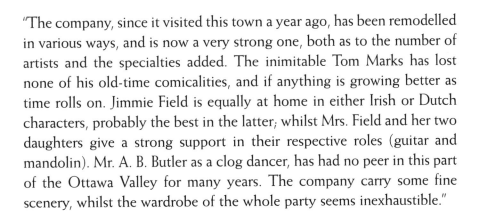

"The company, since it visited this town a year ago, has been remodelled in various ways, and is now a very strong one, both as to the number of artists and the specialties added. The inimitable Tom Marks has lost none of his old-time comicalities, and if anything is growing better as time rolls on. Jimmie Field is equally at home in either Irish or Dutch characters, probably the best in the latter; whilst Mrs. Field and her two daughters give a strong support in their respective roles (guitar and mandolin). Mr. A. B. Butler as a clog dancer, has had no peer in this part of the Ottawa Valley for many years. The company carry some fine scenery, whilst the wardrobe of the whole party seems inexhaustible."

On October 17, the Marks Brothers opened a week's engagement at the Town Hall in Perth, and a local newspaper reporter seated in the audience made the following observations regarding the improved nature of the company's presentations and the quality of its scenery and props:

> "... Tom Marks supported by a well-balanced company produced his new play 'Barney Casey's Luck.' With its realistic and intensely humorous pictures of rural life and variety of scene and incident proved highly satisfactory to the audience. The specialties introduced during the play were first class and were all encored. The flour mill scene, with the large waterwheel in motion in the third act was the finest ever seen here."[1]

As evidenced by the these reviews, Emma Wells and Jennie Ray were not included in the company during the summer and fall of 1893.

Early in their careers R.W. and Tom had learned the importance of cultivating a good rapport with newspaper editors and theatre managers. Over the years these contacts proved invaluable, and the latter kind especially so. Strained relations with theatre managers could prove a death knell for any touring company, as most managers also acted as booking agents. Newspapermen, for the most part, were the community watchdogs, much as they are today. Their editorials and reviews could mean the difference between a successful engagement or near bankruptcy. It was, therefore, paramount that theatrical producers remain within the expected bounds of propriety and good taste with regard to their productions and off-stage activities.

In order to more fully promote the company's talents and entertainments, it was the producer's policy, and R.W. was no exception, to assign an individual, usually the advance agent or musical director to write advertisement copy or even the occasional theatrical review which would prove, needless to say, complimentary. However, this practice was particularly galling to the public. These notices were given to theatre managers who fed them to newspaper editors, and were usually treated by them as genuine critical reports extolling the virtues of the troupe. The public felt cheated because there were many more "rotten shows" than good ones on the road. There was a certain security for proprietors of sub-standard companies in the knowledge that the engagements were short, one or two nights, and each town could be deluded by false advertising before any objective criticism reached them from neighbouring towns.[2]

The year 1894 dawned like most others for R.W. and Tom and, now that Tom had his own company, the two were criss-crossing Ontario, Michigan, Pennsylvania and New York State with great regularity. It was not uncommon for townspeople in these areas to see one Marks' company board a train after concluding a week's engagement while the other disembarked. During this period, from time to time, both companies would unite and tour as one.

Tom's wife, Ella, had now become an integral part of the company, a fact which is not surprising considering she was an accomplished pianist and a deft hand at scoring musical adaptations of plays and illustrated songs. Ella, thanks to her mother, had show business in her blood. The latter having been an actress of some renown who performed under the stage name of Fannie Delmaine.[3]

R.W. and Alex continued their partnership as rumours circulated throughout the industry (started by R.W.) that a third Marks' company was to be formed later that year, but this was not the case. It would be another seven years before the third company, under the management of Joe Marks, would become a reality.

While R.W. and Tom, along with their respective companies, were traversing the countryside on both sides of the border, brothers, Joseph and Mack, were content to remain at Christie Lake and indulge in the pleasures that such a tranquil existence provided. Ernie, at this time, was still in school. Although Mack was initially content to spend his early manhood attending to the daily routines required of a farmer, he would, within a few short years, sell his agricultural holdings and join his brothers; but not on the stage. He, like Alex, preferred the role of advance agent to that of actor.

Joseph, however, had loftier ideals and goals and, in 1894, had accepted the "calling." Most of his waking hours were spent acquiring the knowledge that would one day result in his ordination as an Anglican minister. As fate would have it, this was not to be, for the footlights of the "kerosene circuit" held a far greater appeal; and in light of his brothers overwhelming success this attraction was hardly surprising. The promise of fame and fortune, coupled with the presence of starlet, Grace Andrews, no doubt made his decision to forsake "the cloth" that much easier. The love of Joe's life, for their is no indication of any romantic involvement prior to his meeting her, was born, Mabel Grace Marintha Andrews, circa 1880, at Grand Rapids, Michigan. This charming *soubrette* first performed under the stage name of Gracie Purdue and specialized in child roles. The soon-to-be Mrs. Joseph Marks, was a lady possessed of fine features and physical proportions which remained with her for most of her acting career.

In March 1894, Joseph went to Toronto, probably to continue his ecclesiastical studies. He was not expected to return until late summer. His stay, however, lasted only two months, indicating perhaps that one or more of his brothers had finally convinced him that his destiny lay with the stage and not the pulpit.

Having returned to Christie Lake, Joseph revelled in his favourite pastimes of horse-racing, fishing, hunting and sailing. As mentioned previously, horse-racing was a popular recreation of Tom's, but brothers Joseph, Alex, Mack, R.W. and Ernie were similarly smitten by the sounds of pounding hooves and the financial rewards that awaited a shrewd and knowledgeable punter.

The first week of June saw the arrival of R.W. and Alex at Christie Lake, following a forty-week tour. Tom and his wife, Ella, had also completed their circuit by this time and were spending a few weeks with friends and relatives in the Wingham area. But the remainder of Tom's company were spending the off-season in the United States, giving one the impression that the majority, if not all his players were American.

Now that Emma Wells and Jennie Ray were no longer officially associated with either R.W.'s or Tom's company, they had out of necessity, formed their own company and were giving concerts and recitals at church functions, social clubs and small town fairs. But for some inexplicable reason, during the summer and fall of 1894, the foursome once again combined their talents, as they would do on several occasions in the future. The *Perth Expositor* took note of these unusual circumstances:

> "The Emma Wells Comedy Quartette opened their week's engagement
> in this town Monday night to a packed house. They surprised their
> many friends..."[4]

At the end of October the quartette disbanded. Tom opened at the Victoria Hall in Brockville, while R.W. toured the upper reaches of the Ottawa Valley. It is assumed that Emma Wells and Jennie Ray continued to play their limited circuit, as information regarding their whereabouts is not available. Tom played Brockville for two nights and one matinee; and long before the curtain rose on the first act opening night, standing room was at a premium, and many more would-be patrons were turned away at the door. The first play he presented was the popular Irish drama "Cruiskeen Lawn," but under a different name, "Dublin Dan." The following evening Tom entertained his audience with the drama, "A Legal Wrong" and the comedy farce, "A Rash Marriage," along with the usual accompaniment of singing, dancing, comical recitations and sketches.

Altering the titles of well known contemporary plays and productions in order to circumvent copyright laws was a standard practice in the industry and would remain so for many years.

> "Some of the plays seem to have been ordered especially by Robert Marks, and were performed by his company. But the titles and plots are of such a general nature that it is difficult to view them as original. 'The Little Minister,' for example, was written specifically for Bob Marks, but it is a far cry from the play of the same name by James Barrie. Nor did the Marks' property, 'The Village Blacksmith,' bear any relation to W. S. Gilbert's widely known play. The use of familiar titles was good business. Indeed, most of the plays which were presumably the property of R.W. Marks have a suspicious familiarity about them."[5]

Following Brockville, Tom and his company booked a week's engagement in Perth, before joining forces with R.W., who was scheduled to perform in Ottawa from the third of December to the eighth of December 1894. This was not the first time the Marks brothers had taken their show to the capitol city, but their previous booking dates are unknown. They opened this stand, according to a later statement from the future Mrs. R.W. Marks (May A. Bell), at the Russell Theatre. This, in fact, would have taken a miracle to accomplish, for at that time, the theatre had yet to be built. When the Russell finally opened its doors in 1897, it was lauded as the most opulent facility of its kind between Montreal and Toronto, offering sophisticated audiences the best entertainment available. This mark of quality was a point that May Bell Marks would have quickly seized upon to demonstrate that R.W's company offered superior entertainment, even at popular prices.

Under the circumstances, May A. Bell Marks cannot be chastised for stretching the truth a little, in light of the theatre's excellent reputation for engaging first-rate legitimate theatre companies and its enviable position as being the cultural centre of Ottawa. In reality, the Marks Brothers staged their Ottawa performance in a nondescript building situated at the corner of Bank and Sparks streets above Grant's Furniture Store. Grant's Hall, as it was known, catered to the masses and provided a style

A promising leading lady "par excellence," May A. Bell had made numerous stage appearances
in the United States, primarily New York City, before coming to Ottawa in 1894.
A remarkably versatile performer, she was truly a "queen of the stage." *Perth Museum Collection.*

of entertainment peculiar to their tastes – the type of entertainment the Marks Brothers had been providing for the past eighteen years.

> "Marks' Bros. Musical Dramatic Co., better known in Ottawa as the Emma Wells' Co., begin a week's engagement in Grant's new concert hall, corner Sparks and Bank Streets. December 3 to 8. Admission 10 cents, reserved seats 15 cents."[6]

Four years later, in 1898, shortly after R.W. and his company completed a week's stand, the building was razed by fire.

R.W.'s involvement with Emma Wells both in the personal and theatrical sense were nearing an end, but they would still combine their expertise and talents for several more bookings. However, a business transaction in 1896 would forever seal their fate and result in Miss Wells exiting stage left ... never to be heard from again.

As their personal relationship had been deteriorating for some time, foremost in R.W's mind was finding an experienced actress with enough talent who could quickly replace Emma Wells as leading lady. But decorum and good business practice dictated he should make his enquiries discretely. In his mind, when a suitable candidate was found, it would be necessary to relegate her to supporting roles until the right opportunity arose. Then and only then, she would be brought to the forefront.

On December 5, 1894, two days after R.W and Tom opened at Grant's Hall, they were joined by twenty-three-year-old actress, May A. Bell, from Brooklyn, New York. Although he may not have known it at the time, R.W. had found his leading lady, but she had only been contracted to play for two weeks. It would seem likely that R.W. had met this aspiring New York actress on one of the many sojourns he made to that city in the past.

May Adelaide Bell, was born at seven o'clock in the morning, August 20, 1871, in a house on Hope Street, Brooklyn, the daughter of a stove salesman, Thomas Luther Bell. Her formative education was acquired at the Second Street Public School, before attending the local high school. Hers was an extremely religious Methodist family, in which one uncle had been a minister at the South Second Street Methodist Episcopal Church. Her aunt, Mrs. George Bell, had been an evangelist.

May's volatile emotionalism, for which she would soon earn a nation-wide reputation, was credited as having come from her mother's side of the family – from them she was of French descent. Her ancestry stemmed from the old aristocratic Chauernuff family of France, the patriarch being a government official in Marseilles and, unfortunately for both him and his family, a Huguenot. At the time of the religious

Since 1892, Emma Wells had been R.W.'s leading lady and had even purchased property at Christie Lake, but things were changing. A business arrangement in 1896 would end both their personal and professional relationships. *Perth Museum Collection.*

persecutions (circa 1815), the women of the family were desecrated; but through the aid of some sympathetic townspeople, Chauernuff and two of his sons escaped aboard a ship destined for America.

Soon after their arrival in the United States, one of the sons fell in love with a girl who, records would suggest, was named Mary. She was considered a commoner in the eyes of the elder Chauernuff, who still held fast to the old aristocratic ideals. When the two married, against his father's wishes, the elder Chauernuff and his remaining son left for other parts of the continent and were never heard from again.

On her father's side, May's grandmother was the second cousin to Andrew Jackson, the seventh president of the United States. When left a widow, her grandmother, managed to raise eleven children, May's father being among them. Thomas, who was born June 6, 1845, along with three of his brothers served in the Union Army during the American Civil War. He enlisted as a drummer, and eventually left the service as a ranking soldier.

On May 26, 1868, three years after the end of the War, Thomas Bell married eighteen-year-old, Mary Burras, at the Calvary Church in Brooklyn. Sixteen years later, on November 15, 1884, May's younger sister, Mildred Estelle was born.

Thomas Bell's life-long occupation, that of stove salesman, must have been one that accorded him immense satisfaction along with some measure of financial security and notoriety. At the time of his death on January 22, 1903, at age fifty-eight, the doleful news was placarded about the streets of Brooklyn in a manner befitting royalty.

Acting had not always been May's first choice of professions, for in later years she would reflect:

> "In looking back over the past, and I had my life to live over again, I would have become an evangelist."[7]

Since early childhood she had always shown a marked ability as an elocutionist and took part in church plays and recitations whenever the opportunity arose. When her mother passed away in 1890, May was nineteen years-old, married and pregnant.

On July 20, 1887, she had married George B. Whitman, of whom little is known. Three years later on December 13, 1890, a son was born to the young couple at their Division Street home in Brooklyn. He was christened, George William Whitman.

Soon after the birth of their son, May turned her attentions to the stage, in spite of the horrified protestations of the family who viewed the theatre as a den of sin and iniquity. Why May "took to the boards" instead of pursuing a career as an evangelist will forever remain mystery, but we do know her professional theatrical debut took place in

1891 in Brooklyn, at the Lee Avenue Academy of Music.

This, her first stock engagement, lasted for thirty-seven weeks and although the name of the production has been all but forgotten, cast members included Chester Devonds, who went on to write *Cargo* along with Edward Ames and Frank Tannerhill. May obviously showed great promise in her first role, for at the end of the Brooklyn engagement, the company went on the road and played another thirty-seven weeks at the Kensington Theatre in Philadelphia, where the plays "Michael Stragoff," "Waiting For The Verdict," and "Passion's Slave" were presented.

One evening during a performance of "Passion's Slave," May took seriously ill, but keeping with the true spirit of her profession, and despite her malady, continued in the role. At the final curtain she collapsed and was rushed to St. Mary's Hospital. These were the days before medicare and universal medical plans – a time when extended hospital stays or a lengthy illness could, and often did, result in great financial hardship for the afflicted. To help alleviate May's financial burden, the well-known theatrical producer, Thomas Albee, who was also in Philadelphia at the time, ordered his company to give a benefit performance for the ailing starlet. She received four hundred dollars.

Upon recovery, May resumed her acting career, but on a limited scale, playing only minor roles with several stock companies. Between the all too infrequent bookings she appeared in vaudeville, teaming up with Madam Yucca, "the strong woman." During her performance Madam Yucca would juggle weights before leading up to her finale, the hoisting of a 1,600-pound horse off the floor. Then, May, weighing all of ninety pounds would follow her with song and acrobatic routines.

May's next booking took her back to New York City, followed by a return engagement in Philadelphia. While in New York, she performed in the $10,000 production of "In The Foothills." When the show closed, she auditioned and won a singing part in "Hannel," for which she was to receive a salary of eighty dollars a week once the show opened. The production was slated for the Fifth Avenue Theatre; for three months the cast rehearsed at their own expense. The play was produced by the Rosenfield brothers and directed by Theodore Roberts, who in later years went on to have a successful career in silent movies. Other cast members included Mary Ryan, who eventually married the celebrated theatrical producer Samuel Harris. As well, Emmet Corrigan and Charles B. Richmond, who also appeared in the smash hit "Bought And Paid For," were part of the production.

The play was destined to be a lavish one, complete with graphic sets depicting Heaven and Purgatory. But the insertion of these scenes caused considerable consternation among church-goers who labelled the production sacrilegious. "Hannel" ran for only a week before the cast was given two weeks salary and the production closed. This heart-wrenching episode made May A. Bell a loyal and life-long exponent of Actors' Equity.

May A. Bell (later May A. Bell Marks) must have been a photographer's delight, judging from the many publicity shots that make up an impressive part of the Marks memorabilia collection housed at the Perth Museum in Eastern Ontario. *Perth Museum Collection.*

Robert William (R.W.) Marks was an imposing muscular figure, standing about 6 feet, 2 inches in height. He was described as a sound businessman and a strict parent. The eldest of the Marks brothers, R.W. and his siblings were reputed to have made a profit of over half a million dollars out of melodrama and to have played to upwards of eight million cash customers in Canada and the United States.

CHAPTER 6

ROBERT WILLIAM MARKS – LARGER THAN LIFE KING OF REPERTOIRE

The year 1895 was, in every sense of the word, anti-climactic to the events of 1894, with two exceptions. Firstly, John Jay Marks, the third eldest brother, returned to Christie Lake from Seal Bay, Alaska, on April 25, for the first time in nine years. Secondly, it was the year in which May A. Bell was receiving national acclaim as the "first lady of Canadian popular theatre." Since joining R.W.'s company in Ottawa the year before, she had managed to parlay a two week contract into one that was now open-ended. Having shown her worth, she rose rapidly from playing insignificant supporting roles to that of leading lady.

Since the beginning of the year, R.W. and company had been touring Ontario and the northern reaches of the United States, while Tom had opted to play Western Canada. R.W. concluded the 1894-95 season in early May and returned to the lake, soon to be followed by Tom, Ella and their infant daughter, Arlie. Emma Wells and Jennie Ray, who had been in Toronto, also returned to their property at the lake despite the increasingly more sour relationship with the Marks Brothers. Following a few days of rest and relaxation, R.W. and Tom began making preparations for a trip to New York City.

In the meantime, Ernie, the youngest member of the family, had successfully completed his public school education and was making plans to attend the Perth Collegiate Institute in the fall. In celebration of Ernie's scholastic achievements and John's return home, a week long party was held at the rehearsal hall in early June.

By month's end, however, it was back to business, as R.W. and Tom took the best acts from their respective companies and toured Renfrew County for ten days. On July 10,

R.W. made a flying trip to Ogdensburg, New York, in order to secure accommodation for two week's rehearsals prior to commencing the 1895-96 season. On August 5, the company, which now comprised of R.W., Tom, his wife Ella, Alex and May A. Bell, along with a number of supporting acts left Perth for Ogdensburg. Eleven days later the troupe returned to Perth for a six day engagement. On August 18, John Jay Marks left Christie Lake for North Dakota, never to return.

Throughout the 1895-96 season the unified company was content to play the Eastern Ontario and northern New York circuit, which also included a two week stint in Ottawa. The troupe was now carrying a myriad of scenery, props and costumes, including drops that depicted an agricultural setting, in addition to street, parlour, kitchen, prison and garden scenes. This vast array of accoutrements were now deemed a necessity as audiences demanded quality, as opposed to quantity, when it came to their theatrical entertainments.

By mid-November, the brothers were again playing the Ottawa Valley towns, and their engagement in Pembroke was hailed by the local newspaper as being their eleventh annual visit. Accompanying the troupe on this sweep were Lee J. Kellam, Myra Collins, Petite Gracie (Whitcher) and, of course, leading lady, May A. Bell. When the company played Perth between December 2 and 7, 1895, it marked the first time May A. Bell appeared in the town before a paying audience. On the previous Perth engagement of mid-August, she was unable to perform due to illness.

During December 1895, and into the new year, R.W. and Tom played the local circuit which had been expanded to include the towns of Brockville and Gananoque. While playing in these locales, newspaper advertisements and reviews referred to the troupe as the Emma Wells Comedy Company, even though Miss Wells was no longer officially associated with the company, and omitted all reference to the Marks Brothers. It is very likely that R.W., in failing to rectify the situation, was capitalizing on the excellent reputation enjoyed by Emma Wells' company.

Another surprising event connected with R.W. and Tom during the year, centred around an April 14 newspaper article in the Toronto *Globe*, which reported the Marks Brothers Comedy Company opened a week's engagement at the Queen Street Theatre on April 13, when they performed "The Paris Detective." This statement contradicts the general believe that the Marks brothers and their companies never played the larger Canadian cities:

> "The Marks boys stayed solvent because they always knew they were
> small-timers, so they stuck to small-time circuits. None of the brothers
> attempted to play Montreal or Toronto. They passed up Winnipeg and

Vancouver when those cities started to grow. They played briefly and rarely in Hamilton and Ottawa. They were wise enough to leave such places to the big English and American road companies, and stay where they were sure of a welcome."[1]

It should be noted that during the 1920s and early 1930s when melodrama was waning, both R.W. and May A. Bell Marks played vaudeville in Montreal and Toronto.

Following this Toronto engagement, R.W. and Tom, along with their players, returned to Christie Lake, as did Emma Wells and Jennie Ray. A few weeks later R.W. travelled to New York City in search of new plays and personnel. When he returned on June 2, he brought with him a new mechanical novelty – Edison's Vitascope (an early motion picture projector.) Later that month, he rented White's schoolhouse in South Sherbrooke township, and entertained local residents with the Vitascope, vaudeville, melodrama and shadowgraphs. The previous evening a similar entertainment had been given in the hamlet of Harper.

Not to be outdone by R.W.'s new mechanical novelty, Tom devised his own, method of generating income which he put into practice on June 23, 1896, the day appointed for the Dominion elections. He, along with Robert Burris, a fellow actor, acquired permission from the local returning officer to read the nightly election results from the stage in the Perth Town Hall. This they would do for a small admission fee of ten cents; and those residents who chose to partake in the evening's festivities were treated to a night of song, dance and mirth during the extended intermissions when ballots were being counted.

In early August, R.W. and Tom took their thirteen-member company, which now included Alex, Joseph and Ella Marks, James R. Field, Gertrude Field, Alice Kemp, Hattie Van Buren, May A. Bell, Petite Gracie, Charles McKinley and Ned Curtis, to Alexandria Bay, New York. Here, they spent four weeks in rehearsals followed by engagements in Brockville and Gananoque, where they performed "Jerry and the Tramp," "Lost Heirs" and "The Waif of the Mines."

On September 14, the troupe returned to Perth and played for five days at the Town Hall. Throughout their long careers the Marks brothers were proud to proclaim:

"No bailiff ever sat on our trunks, and we never missed a payroll."[2]

But the same could not be said for other touring companies and, in particular, The Cook Brothers' Company, which played Smiths Falls on September 11, 1896. Their trouble, however, was not with the local bailiff, but with a gentleman of far more

By 1895, May A. Bell was already receiving national recognition as the "first lady of Canadian popular theatre." She would remain the headliner for the Marks Brothers until her retirement. *Perth Museum Collection.*

imposing authority – the Chief of Police. The Cook Brothers, whose real names were Harry and David Arpin, of Montana, fled Smiths Falls aboard a Montreal-bound train during the early morning hours of September 12. Behind them they left their players penniless and unable to pay for either food or lodgings. When this dastardly deed first came to light, the grieved parties notified the authorities and, subsequently, charges of deceit and falsehood with intent to defraud, and theft of stage fixtures were laid against the two men.

Once it was learned they were making their way to Montreal, Chief Gavin, of the Smiths Falls Police Department, telegraphed the Montreal police advising them of the charges awaiting the two in his community. The "long arm of the law" sprang into action and, within four hours, the Arpin brothers were arrested; and while shackled hand and foot they loudly proclaimed their innocence. Both Harry and David adamantly declared it had not been their intention to cheat or defraud anyone – they had just simply run out of money. According to David, their flight had been one of necessity and was designed to procure sufficient funds which would allow them to meet their financial obligations.

On September 23, the Arpin brothers appeared at the Perth Courthouse (the county seat) before Judge W.W. Senklar. Here, they recounted their woeful tale. The court was told the company had arrived in Smiths Falls on Friday morning and booked into the Russell House. That evening the troupe was scheduled to play the local opera house, but as the curtain time drew closer, attendance was less than expected and gate receipts were minimal.

The principal witnesses for the prosecution were members of the troupe who sought to show that the success of the company, prior to the Smiths Falls engagement, was so great that the prisoners had on hand between them at least four hundred dollars. Their evidence, however, was not convincing and carried little weight with the judge. Further examination only served to show that in reality, the prisoners must indeed have been destitute and, ultimately, all charges against the brothers were dropped. Needless to say, the company never appeared again in Eastern Ontario, anyways, not under the name of Cook or Arpin brothers.

Meanwhile, the Marks brothers were busily engaged in fulfilling their Eastern Ontario engagements. On October 5, they began a successful two week booking in Pembroke, before going on to play other communities in the district. While playing Almonte, the first week in November, word reached them of Jennie's untimely death in Toronto. Jennie passed away on October 22, of an undisclosed illness. Following Almonte, the troupe performed in Smiths Falls for a week.

After her sister's death, Emma Wells began making preparations to leave Christie

This scene from the "The Point of the Sword," a third act of the Marks Brothers No. 1 Company production during the 1895-1896 season, features May A. Bell in the starring role. In this play, one of their most popular melodramas, she takes the part of a gypsy queen who is really a kidnapped nobleman's daughter. The Marks Brothers' melodramas always had a happy ending as the gallery patrons hissed the "villain" to oblivion. *Perth Museum Collection.*

Lake for good. In doing so, she would sever all ties with R.W. and other Marks family members. There is little doubt that Jennie's death weighed heavily on Emma's mind, and therefore played an instrumental role in her decision; but R.W.'s budding romance with May A. Bell also added to her resolution that a parting of the ways would benefit all. In early December, she begrudgingly sold her Christie Lake property, "Red Cedar Wild," to R.W. for six hundred dollars. From this date on, nothing more would be heard from the lady who had played an integral part in R.W.'s early theatrical career and who was, in some respects, responsible for his overall success.

Their parting, however, was not a cordial one. Family history records that Emma, in a fit of rage and frustration threatened to haunt the shores of Christie Lake, and in particular, "Red Cedar Wild," for as long as R.W. remained there. Due to the very nature of the threat, it is not surprising that no one took her seriously — at least not for the time being.

But an incident thirty years later involving R.W.'s five-year-old niece, rekindled old memories and added an eerie dimension to Emma's parting words of warning. "I was perhaps, five-years-old at the time," remarked Bettie Kelly, daughter of Ernie and Kitty Marks; "when I visited Uncle Robert (R.W.) and Aunt May (May A. Bell Marks) at Red Cedar. On this particular occasion, as I had many times before, I walked from our cottage to my uncle's home. Whenever I visited their home, May would allow me to play in the 'green room;' that's where all the costumes, wigs, jewellery and assorted theatrical equipment was stored. That room was like Aladdin's Cave to a five-year-old. I remember I had a marvellous afternoon there. Later in the day one of my brothers came to take me home." She continued:

> "A week later – as a child it is hard to decipher the difference between a day and a week – I returned to Red Cedar and the 'green room.' Shortly after my arrival, May came in and asked, 'What costume are you wearing today?' to which I replied, 'It's no fun today, there's no little girl to play with me.' She queried me, 'Where's that little girl I heard you talking to the last time you were here?' No doubt she was remembering that she had heard two distinct voices, believing I had brought a young friend with me, one that she hadn't seen at the time. 'I don't know,' was my reply, 'she was here and all ready dressed [in one of the costumes] when I arrived.'
>
> "You should have seen the look of shock and dismay on her then, pale face. I can still see it today [1988]. As I remember, the little girl was attired in an old-fashioned dress, and we laughed and played all afternoon – yet I never saw her again."

Five or six years later another equally mysterious incident left Bettie (Marks) Kelly, and several teenage friends, including her brother Ted, who was killed overseas during World War ll, in a state of frenzy and bewilderment. "One summer's evening, Ted, myself and two or three girl friends, were seated around a table in one of the cottages at Christie Lake; indulging in the esoteric secrets of a Ouija board," remarked Mrs. Kelly.

> "In those days electricity had not yet been installed in most cottages at the lake, and the main source of light came from ceiling-mounted kerosene or coal-oil lamps. As the evening wore on the Ouija board was losing its appeal and fascination. It was then that Ted said, 'Is there

anybody here that shouldn't be?'

"All of a sudden, and for no explicable reason that I can think of, a flame shot from the lamp right up to the ceiling. The flame was so intense that we ran screaming from the room fearful of the consequences should we remain, that is, all but Ted, who was knocked out of his chair. He was just as upset as the rest of us, so there is no doubt in my mind that any of this was his doing.

These incidents had a profound affect on several members of the Marks family. The circumstances surrounding these 'supernatural' occurrences have, over the years, been repeated time and time again; and the same question arises "...had the spirit of Emma Wells truly returned to haunt R.W. and Christie Lake?"

Throughout 1897, the Marks Brothers Dramatic Company, the word comedy having been dropped for the more professional designation, dramatic, was touring Michigan, Minnesota and Northwestern Ontario. The communities of Eastern Ontario and northeastern United States would have to wait until September 1898 before R.W. and Tom would again play in the region. But in the meantime, filling the void left by the Marks Brothers were The Guy Brothers Minstrels, The Dan Allen Company, The Andrews Dramatic Company, The Kickapoo Indian Medicine Company, and a host of other less professional and talented entertainers.

Acting, like other professions, has its share of occupational hazards and, although the Marks Brothers rarely encountered the antics of pistol-packing cowboys during these days, there were other less obvious dangers lurking in the wings. Alex Marks was one actor who fell victim to these theatrical "pitfalls," (he had temporarily abandoned his position of advance agent) when he plunged from stage and landed in the orchestra pit. He was playing the role of a policeman in "Jerry The Tramp" in a small Minnesota town when accident occurred.

The part required Alex to chase the tramp around the rostrum and, once apprehended, struggle with his captive. Right on cue he lunged for the miscreant, but, in doing so, missed his mark and fell head over heels into the orchestra, breaking his ankle. His injury, although painful, was not serious and he returned to work a few weeks later. His speedy recovery was no doubt aided somewhat by the news, garnered through a Perth newspaper, that the Marks family was going to share in $375,000 from the estate of Thomas Farrell, their paternal grandfather, who had passed away a few months earlier.

During the 1897-98 season, the Marks Brothers' Dramatic Company played over ninety weeks in Minnesota, Wisconsin, Michigan and Northwestern Ontario. Individual engagements were now lasting for weeks instead of the usual four or five days. In Sault Ste. Marie, Michigan, the tour of duty lasted five weeks (October 6, to November 12, 1897) with a return date booked for Thanksgiving week. Then it was off for a five day stint in Stillwater, Minnesota, followed by six weeks in Minneapolis. After a short rest the troupe headlined in Duluth, from January 15 to February 5, 1898. During this booking, the Marks Brothers presented twenty-one plays.

Seventeen players now made up the company and included nineteen-year-old Ernie, R.W., Tom, Alex and Joe. In February 1898, the *Minneapolis Tribune* heaped rave reviews on the troupe, which was playing in the capitol, exclaiming that the company was commanding nightly audiences in excess of a thousand people. The overwhelming reception afforded the Marks Brothers in these states only reinforced the declaration made by many newspapers that "...this company had no equal when it came to offering popular theatre at popular prices."

For the most part, those days of having to contend with the rowdy element at performances were almost history. But in one remote Wisconsin community, there was one individual who had either not heard of R.W. and Tom's pugilistic reputation, or foolishly chose to ignore it. But his actions would embroil the "strongman and the wildcat" in a situation that, without the support of the townspeople, could have spelled ruin for the Lanark County showmen. Their ordeal started when a drunk, seated in the front row at one of the performances, insisted on contributing, in a loud and boisterous manner, his own opinions of both the actors and the production. Within seconds of the outburst, R.W. and Tom jumped over the footlights and heaved the heckler into the night.

At the end of the performance, the miscreant, bent on revenge, returned to the "opry house," accompanied by the sheriff. He identified himself as the mayor's brother and insisted that R.W. be charged and arrested for assault. The errant thespian was escorted to the jail and remained there for several days. But when the case came before the local magistrate, certain events had transpired unbeknown to R.W. During his incarceration a bitter feud had broken out which resulted in the whole town taking sides. Many people, including the magistrate, felt the mayor's brother had been attempting to run the town and were overjoyed that, by laying an assault charge against the actor, he had given them a chance to attack him publicly.

The townspeople had quietly collected about forty witnesses for the defence, witnesses who were prepared to testify to all manner of things. The judge took the attitude that the question to be proved was whether R.W. had been guilty of an assault; and why the town bully, with a reputation to uphold, had allowed himself to be man-

May A. Bell Marks with her son, Robert J. Marks in front of their Christie Lake home, later the Red Cedar Inn, circa 1911. *Perth Museum Collection.*

handled by an "unknown" – and an actor at that.

"Why did you let this man throw you out of the hall?" thundered the magistrate.[3]

The troublemaker was taken aback by the question and was equally surprised at the judge's attitude; yet he managed to stammer. "He took me too quick."[4] The case was dismissed amid the laughter of a crowded courtroom.

Joe and Ernie, accompanied by Gracie Whitcher, were the first to arrive at Christie Lake during the 1898 season. They stayed only a few days and on May 2 left Perth for Duluth, intending to join Tom's troupe. Instead, for some reason, they connected with R.W.'s company, in Little Falls, Minnesota, now about to make its way back to Christie Lake. By now Tom was playing in Michigan and southwestern Ontario. While performing in Alpena, Michigan, two members of his company, Herbert K. Betts and Amele Losee, "tied the proverbial knot" and, as Tom was the most senior member of the troupe, he gave away the bride.

On August 17, R.W. left for a two week jaunt to New York City; accompanied by May A. Bell and her seven-year-old son, George. They were on their way to visit family and friends in Brooklyn. When May and George returned to Perth in early September, they had with them, May's fourteen-year-old sister, Millie. She, by now, was also an accomplished actress. While in New York, R.W. met and subsequently hired a native son, Chris Allen. Allen was a talented singer, dancer, comedian and raconteur, and would spend over twenty years with the Marks Brothers, before he and another Marks' prodigy, "Big" Bill Dyer, left in the early 1920s for successful film careers in Hollywood. The troupe was growing both in size and in talent.

On September 17, 1898, R.W. began two weeks of rehearsals at the Perth Town Hall, which was also the starting point, from October 3 to October 8, for the 1898-99 season. R.W.'s company now numbered fourteen players and, following Perth, the troupe headlined in Smiths Falls and Cornwall. During rehearsals on September 23 and 24,

Perth residents were able to take in two "paid pressure practices" when the plays "Chick The Mountain Waif" and "A Soldier's Daughter" were presented. Participating in these productions was May's son, Georgie Whitman, who received several accolades for his performances:

> "Baby George in the Marks Brothers show captivated the Perth audiences at last Friday and Saturday's plays, but more particularly the part he took in the play. How one so young could attain such marked proficiency is a matter of great wonder. One lady in the audience remarked:
> – 'I could just hug the little darling,' and that is about the feeling of many of those present."[5]

George Whitman, in later years, changed his surname to Whitman Marks and he, along with his wife Tiny, would go on to have a successful career in vaudeville and "popular theatre."

May's father, Thomas, had never completely come to grips with her acting career, and had yet to see her perform on stage. When he did, at Watertown, New York, praise was reserved not for his daughter, but for his grandson, George. "I can remember it well," she is quoted as saying. "I was so glad that my father had at last consented to lay aside his prejudice and I decided on that night to act better than I had ever done before. When I got through, I rushed to him all excited and asked, 'How did you like it?' He replied, 'George was splendid wasn't he?'"[6]

During the Perth booking of October 1898, audiences were treated to a potpourri of plays including, "Uncle Tom's Cabin," "A Solider's Daughter," "The Two Orphans," "Under the British Flag," "The Black Flag," "Ten Nights in a Barroom," "A Ticket of Leave," "Little Lord Fauntleroy" and "A Farmer's Daughter."

Earlier that year, September 9, Tom's company had opened a week's engagement in London, Ontario. During the run, the troupe gave a benefit performance for an actor's wife who had fallen on hard times after her husband had been charged and subsequently jailed for murder. The actor, a Mr. Emerson, shot and killed his manager during a heated argument backstage at the London Opera House. He was latter acquitted. At the beginning of September, Tom had played Saginaw, Michigan, where he acquired several new acts including DeVoe and his "Wargraph," Will Mallard, trick bicyclist, and the Crumley Children, a song and dance team.

Following the Cornwall booking in the fall of 1898, R.W. found it necessary to acquire several new players, including Matt McGinnis and J. Knox Gavin. They opened in a two week run beginning November 7 at the Grant's Hall in Ottawa. On opening night over five hundred people were turned away and the remainder of the engagement was equally successful. All performances were standing room only. Many of the male members of the audience were so taken with the performances of May and Millie Bell, that the sisters were presented with numerous floral bouquets as tokens of affection and appreciation.

As the Marks Brothers' fame increased so did their companies. Matt McGinnis, J. Knox Gavin, Agnes Earle, Millie Bell and Albert Denier had now been hired on long term contracts to bolster the troupes.

Following the Ottawa booking, R.W. and company played the Grand Opera House in Brockville, and opened before a veritable sea of spectators. Over one thousand enthusiastic theatre-goers crammed into the hall and according to the *Brockville Recorder*, the Wednesday afternoon matinee was equally well-attended.

> "... 'The Little Duchess' was presented at the matinee and 'A Soldier's Sweetheart' at night. There is not a dull moment in the plays. The characters are natural, the situations ludicrous and the dialogue sparkling. People were obliged to stand all through the show, and money was refunded to many who could not get standing room."[7]

From Brockville, the troupe headed to Kingston. The company opened December 5, at the Grand Opera House on Princess Street. But early the following morning disaster struck when the building caught fire. The blaze broke out about four o'clock and quickly engulfed the premises. An adjacent saloon, tailor's shop and bicycle shop were only partially damaged; and luckily for their owners, the stock and buildings were covered by insurance. The owner of the theatre, however, was not quite so fortunate; for although he carried insurance on the building, he had not deemed it necessary to protect the furniture and furnishings.

When the news of the fire reached R.W. at his hotel, he hurried down to Princess Street and with a heavy heart watched the "dowager dutchess" of Kingston theatre crumble beneath the flames. The following morning, realizing that time was of the essence, he set out in search of local dressmakers. By the time he had finished, ninety-seven seamstresses were diligently engaged in creating new costumes. At the same time R.W. telegraphed New York City and ordered $1,200 worth of scenery and props.

It would appear, however, that the company was no stranger to the ravages of fire:

> "The fire fiend is following the Marks Brothers in earnest. Upon leaving

By 1896, Joe Marks, the fourth brother, had turned away from a career with the Anglican ministry and become part of the family troupe. In 1901, he and Alex would form a third Marks Brothers Company and take to the road. *Perth Museum Collection.*

Ernie Marks, the youngest of the Marks siblings, joined his theatrical brothers when he was 19 years of age. *Perth Museum Collection.*

Grant's Hall, Ottawa, after a two week's engagement the building was burned; recently the Kingston Opera House was burned, and on the last night during the performance in Brockville's Opera House, it is said a fire started in the ladies dressing room, but was extinguished before getting under headway."[8]

As was his usual custom in Kingston, R.W. had leased the Grand for two weeks and had paid the rental fee in advance. Because of the fire, the company was forced to perform in the City Hall for the remainder of the booking. When a final tally had been made, R.W. and cast estimated the loss of costumes, props, scenery and personal effects at $8,500. The losses were as follows: R.W., $2,000; May A. Bell, $1,500; Joe Marks, $900; Ernie Marks, $300; Matt McGinnis, $150; Agnes Earle, $800; Jennie Platt, $1,000; J. Knox Gavin, $600; Albert Denier, $700; Grace Whitcher, $300 and Louis Von Wetheroff, $250. The loss was even more devastating for Von Wetheroff, as he had travelled all the way from Missouri to join the company for opening night.

This remarkable photograph was donated to the Perth Museum by Leonard M. Quinlan of Vermont, USA. Standing at rear (l to r): Joe Marks and Alex Marks. Front (l to r): May A. Bell, her son George Whitman, R.W. Marks, and Gracie Marks (Mrs. Joe Marks), date not known. *Perth Museum Collection.*

The opera house fire, although creating considerable hardships for the company, plus creating a number of logistical problems, was soon forgotten in the wake of a more joyous event – R.W.'s marriage on December 16, to the troupe's leading lady, May A. Bell. May at the time was twenty-seven years old, while R.W. had just turned forty-five a few months earlier. The wedding took place at the Queen Street Methodist Church, Kingston, and was performed by Reverend Jas. Elliot. R.W.'s two sisters, Nellie and Olivia, travelled from Christie Lake for the occasion, while brothers, Joe and Ernie, along with other company members also attended the ceremony. The *Perth Expositor* made note about R.W.'s fortunes of late:

> "...Mr. Marks is an able manager and he got for his wife a lady who will no doubt bring him as much success and happiness in that capacity as she has done as an actress; Mr. Marks himself has shown that he possesses no ordinary amount of nerve and energy by his management after the recent fire, but his taking so important a step in life so soon after his heavy loss by fire caps the climax. He is evidently in need of sympathy...."[9]

One can only surmise the writer of this article was referring to R.W.'s misfortunes incurred by the fire and not his marriage. The *Whig-Standard* of Kingston, when reporting their union, mentioned that the city had always been a place of great interest for the new bride, insomuch as it was the first place she appeared in Canada while playing with Harry Lindley's Company. However, May A. Bell Marks never once mentioned this fact in any of her numerous interviews that were given during the next thirty-four years.

Harry Lindley, like R.W., was a well known actor and producer who was particularly identified in Eastern Ontario with Ottawa's Grant Hall. Lindley's real name was Woodwall. A native of Ireland, he had been educated in Dublin for the priesthood. When hostilities between the American north and south culminated in a civil war, he gave up his religious studies, sailed for the United States and fought for the south. When the war was over, Lindley, defeated but not conquered, joined a band of strolling players, one of the many which had travelled from camp-to-camp entertaining the troops. About 1898, Lindley played for a number of months in Vancouver. If May A. Bell Marks had once been a member of his troupe, it would have been prior to 1894, the year she joined R.W.'s troupe in Ottawa.

R.W. and May's only son, Robert J. Marks, who passed away at Perth in 1988, maintained in a 1979 interview:

"My father saw a Harry Lindley show. She (May A. Bell) was dancing for him. He (R.W.) got his eye on her and went backstage afterwards and said, 'I'd like you to come with me next year,' and she said 'well okay,' the salary was alright, and she did. And then he went down to New York and asked her if she'd marry him and she said 'Okay, I guess, we'll see."[10]

Tom, who was touring Western Ontario, was unable to attend the ceremony. His poor health, due to a number of severe sciatica attacks, forced him to leave the company at St. Marys in early December, while he sought relief at a spa in Mount Clemens, Michigan.

A honeymoon was out of the question for the newlyweds because of R.W.'s contractual agreements. The troupe was required to play Smiths Falls, Carleton Place and Almonte before the end of the month.

During the winter of 1899, Mack Marks was still content to remain at Christie Lake, but gradually he was gravitating towards a theatrical career, although he may not have known it at the time. Mack took the first step on Friday, February 3, when he, along with David Anderson, took it upon themselves to organize a dance at the lake.

R.W., at this time, was still playing the local circuit, while Tom, (who had recovered from his ailment) and Alex toured Michigan and the surrounding states. As the years went by, it became apparent that R.W. preferred to remain closer to Christie Lake than he had done in the past.

Although Tom's company was playing under a tight schedule, Alex still took time out to become the fourth Marks brother to "take the plunge." The exact date of his marriage is not known, but we do know he married a Miss Anglin, a

A later theatrical still of George Whitman Marks and his wife, Tiny, often billed as The Marks Duo, not dated. *Perth Museum Collection.*

fellow trouper in the company, at Kalamazoo, Michigan, sometime between January and March 1899. Perhaps, this Miss Anglin was Margaret Anglin, a member of a distinguished Canadian family, who first saw the light of day in the Speakers' Chambers at the House Commons. In 1914, she undertook to produce a successful series of plays from the Greek classics. She later produced a series of Shakespearean comedies, thereby establishing herself as the leading female exponent of the classic drama in America.

In mid-April, Tom, along with Alex and his bride, arrived at the lake after closing the season. They remained there until late May when they left for Sault Ste. Marie. It should be noted that Alex's wife is never mentioned again either by the Marks' family members or the media; leaving one to speculate that theirs was not a happy marriage which may have ended in a quick separation. Today, surviving members of the Marks family believe that Alex remained a bachelor all his life. To some degree this is true, for he never remarried.

From May 8 to 13, 1899, R.W. and company played Barrie; but two days into the booking, tragedy struck. Alexander Furniss, a twenty-four-year-old supporting actor in the troupe, who was reported to be from an old and distinguished English family, decided to go fishing in his spare time. During those hours of relaxation, the young man caught a bad cold and died. The cost of burying Furniss was borne by R.W., a responsibility he assumed without hesitation.

A few days later, on Thursday, May 18, R.W., supported by Tom and Alex, began a week long booking in Perth. Although the community was in the clutches of a torrential downpour for several days, it did not deter the townspeople from filling the hall to capacity every night.

> "...Robert W. Marks has around him one of the strongest companies visiting Perth in years. May A. Bell Marks is in all leading roles and a decided success. Jennie Platt and J. Knox Gavin are as popular as ever and their singing is much appreciated. Fred C. Wilson is one of the most natural comedians on the stage. Chris Allen and Matt McGinnis in their positions are all right. Petite Gracie has lost none of her popularity. Little George is a wonder, nothing short of it. Alice Kemp makes a splendid Irish girl and Mr. Franklin, pianist shows much talent. Joe Marks also takes his parts in good style.
>
> "The wardrobe of the ladies of the company is a very expensive and elaborate one, and the diamonds worn by May A. Bell Marks on some occasions are valued at nearly $5,000."[11]

Tom opened at Sault Ste. Marie in mid-June and played the region until the first week of October, when he was joined by R.W.'s company for a return engagement. But prior to this, R.W. dismissed the company on May 24 and resolved to spend the next three months at Christie Lake. After the company disbanded, Millie Bell left Perth for Brooklyn and, when she returned in mid-July, she was accompanied by her father, Thomas Bell. This would be the first and only time May's father would come to the lake.

On September 7, 1899, R.W., May A. Bell Marks, Georgie, Millie Bell, Ernie and Joe Marks boarded a train in Perth for Mount Clemens, where they connected with Tom and Alex. Missing from the company on this swing was Gracie Whitcher, who had since joined a company formed by her father and a Mr. Machan. This new addition on the theatrical circuit had been fashioned purely on the strength of Gracie's popularity and, although she was a competent actress, she possessed neither the talent nor the expertise to lead a touring company. When Gracie opened in Perth on October 16 she received more than satisfactory reviews, but neither the good reviews nor the company would last very long.

Probably the most imaginative rumour circulating throughout Perth during the autumn of 1899, intimated that John Jay Marks, when, and if he returned from the Klondike where he was mining for gold, would form the third Marks' company. "The gold mine for him may be much nearer home," was a phrase bantered around the beverage rooms in the community, where those men who had once entertained the idea of seeking their fortune in the inhospitable climate that was the Canadian North West Territory, whiled away the hours.

The fifth Marks son, Alex, was the next to marry, to a Miss Anglin, sometime in early 1899. The union was short-lived, but Alex was never to remarry. *Perth Museum Collection.*

On board a steamer on Georgian Bay, heading for an engagement in Parry Sound.
It is believed that this group was part of the Joe Marks company.
Photo is from an album compiled by Joe and Gracie Marks, not dated. *Courtesy Doug Bell.*

CHAPTER 7

LIFE ON THE ROAD

Life on the road even at the turn of the enlightened twentieth century was no "bed of roses." Rapid transportation was virtually non-existent; the early trains along with the traditional horse and wagon would still remain the primary source of locomotion during the early 1900s. But promptness and dependability regarding these modes of conveyance were, for the most part, only words in a dictionary.

Whenever possible, train travel was preferred, but much depended on one's destination and time of year as to the speed and quality of service. This was especially obvious when journeying through the upper reaches of Ontario and the western provinces, where commuters were frequently at the mercy of inclement weather and inhospitable terrain. Equipment breakdowns were forever playing havoc with already loose timetables. It was not uncommon for passengers to be stranded for hours or even days while workmen cleared fallen debris or snow from the tracks, or toiled fervently to repair an out-of-date or overworked locomotive.

Upon completion of the transcontinental Canadian Pacific Railway in 1885, those communities not fortunate enough to find themselves situated in close proximity to the main "iron road" often waited in vain for a promised branch or spur line. But many of these small towns and villages were of a size and nature that constituted the Marks' Brothers "bread and butter."

Necessity dictated the company should disembark at the nearest terminal and, with the assistance of an advance agent, hire a buckboard and wagon to transport the company, props, scenery and the all-important piano to the local music hall. In later years as communities became more affluent, they usually purchased their own piano, which allowed R.W. to relegate his instrument to a prominent position at Red Cedar Inn.

When the eminent English actor, Sir John Martin-Harvey, toured Canada in 1914, he found winter train travel on the prairies much to his liking — perhaps:

> "The play is over, we have returned to our hotel, gathered up our suitcases, which hold the necessities for a night journey, and motor to the railway depot. Our departure will often be delayed to enable the working staff to catch it. They will arrive at any time between 1 am and 3 am; it depends upon the amount of scenery which has to be taken down and transported to the depot...The outline of the two sleeping cars guides us to our quarters for the night...You get a glimpse of other passengers furred to the eyes in shaggy raccoon or beaver coats, hurrying across the tracks to get into the comfortable interiors; your berth with snowy sheets and rugs of old Indian pattern, looks very inviting.
>
> "At least six pillows wedge you in from any possible draught, and storm rugs hung across the windows will keep you warm; if too warm there is an electric fan which you can start from your bed...The green curtains concealing the berths in the sleeper make a long green corridor down the coach. The boots of the occupants protrude beneath. They may have feet in them, so tread cautiously! These belong to the ladies who are performing elaborate acrobatic feats in trying to undress in a sitting position."[1]

In later years Ernie's wife, Kitty, would recall the hardships endured by players as they made their way from town to town in over-crowded railway cars. It was not uncommon, she noted, after catching an early morning train to see cast members meandering up and down the coach, rehearsing their lines while children slept or played in the aisles.

> "I travelled with my parents until I was four years of age," remarked Bettie (Marks) Kelly, Ernie and Kitty's daughter. "I can remember my mother telling me that I didn't have any toys to play with because there just wasn't room for doll carriages, dolls and tea sets. So I made my own toys on those long train trips. I would go to each lady in the company, in those days they carried velvet bags that hung from the wrist. I would

A later more modern form of transportation for members of Joe's troupe in Grand Rapids, Michigan, taken from Joe and Gracie Marks' album, not dated. *Courtesy Doug Bell.*

borrow these bags and turn them upside down on the seat and very carefully put the contents back, examining each article as it was returned. These were my toys."[2]

Touring companies travelling through the Canadian hinterland often found themselves in the unenviable position of waiting for trains that never arrived. Such no-shows would result in a financial loss for the company manager, actors and theatre owner alike. A typical scenario depicting these unforeseen hazards, and one which Tom Marks no doubt faced when he toured the mining and logging towns of British Columbia, would unfold as described in the following:

At 7:30 in the morning, the company would be at the train station ready for the next "jump" (the journey from one town to the next.) In theatrical lingo, performing a week's engagement was known "breaking the jump." The advance agent has left an itinerary saying the next stand is in Rossland, British Columbia, at four o'clock in the afternoon. The seven-thirty train arrives at the Hedley station at eleven-thirty in the

The wait goes on - Tom Marks and Co.

morning, with a connecting train to Rossland leaving from the same depot at one pm, which by all accounts would allow the troupe to arrive in town in plenty of time for the afternoon matinee.

While waiting on the platform, an announcement is made that the train has been delayed for two hours. This means one has to pass the time by smoking, talking or reading. Once the train arrives, it continues to lose time due to an ever-increasing snowfall, which plays havoc on the nerves for fear of missing the Rossland connection. The train finally pulls in at two-thirty in the afternoon and all are reassured by the station master saying, "You will arrive on time if all goes well." One soon comes to the realization that all has not gone well and no train will arrive that day.

When the company finally arrived at its destination, it was usually met by the advance agent who would escort the players to the hotel or boarding house he had chosen. The daily routine seldom changed. After having settled in at their lodgings, the company would go to the hall, where the men unloaded the equipment needed for the engagement. In many cases this would necessitate hauling props, sets, costume trunks

Putting in time at the station...

and other assorted bundles up a long flight of stairs to the second floor where the entertainment would be given.

Here they would hang and arrange scenery, tack-up sets, test the lighting and unpack trunks. Within an hour or two the stage was set. Then it was time for a quick lunch followed by a matinee performance.

In some instances the halls and opera houses were far too small to accommodate all the company's props and sets. Consequently, so much of it remained on the wagon or propped-up against the building to face the onslaught of the elements. And there were times when it became necessary to borrow furniture from local undertakers, who as a rule, owned the town's only furniture store.

Waiting with the trunks...

These photographs are from albums compiled by Joe and Gracie Marks.
Courtesy Doug Bell.

After supper it was back to the hall to prepare for the evening's performance – sorting out costumes and slapping on make-up. Immediately after the show, if it was not a one-night stand, the cast returned to their rooms, where they listened to the stage director's ideas and criticisms. These sessions often lasted well into the early morning hours.

> "On more than one winter's night, the male members of the company took turns tending the stoves all night in rooming houses and hotels to keep warm. There was no breakfast in bed – no basket of roses awaiting you in the dressing room," remarked Kitty Marks in a 1958 interview.[3]

Actors and actresses were not always considered welcomed guests in many hotels, and the management would often go to great lengths to ensure their stay was not as pleasant as it could be.

Tom Marks and his stock company on the road in the west, circa 1903. It has been said they were the first entertainers to perform in the prairie country. *Courtesy Doug Bell.*

While playing in a western town, a regular stop on the circuit, Tom encountered the usual apathy afforded actors. His stature as a prominent showman had little effect on the local innkeeper – a situation all the Marks' companies would encounter at sometime or another. At this stage in Tom's career he could well-afford to stay in the best hotels and, whenever possible, he did so.

Most halls and opera houses in which the Marks Brothers played during the early years were nothing more than barn-like structures which lacked the most rudimentary facilities. Dressing rooms were virtually non-existent. There were no full length mirrors or electric lights, on the contrary, if a dressing room was available, it was usually a drab and dreary affair where light emanated from dusty oil lamps, and floors were often constructed of rough planking with gaping holes that were home to all manner of vermin. Blankets thrown over unused props were, more often than not, all that comprised a dressing room.

George Nelson Janes, another prominent thespian playing the "kerosene circuit" spent much of his early career playing one night stands in small-town Canada. During his extensive career he had several harrowing experiences which today have a comic ring about them:

> "Dressing room space, to say the least, is limited in the small theatre. Usually, space in the wings serves the purpose.
>
> "In one hall we played the wings were open to view. As there was no other dressing room space we hung white sheets between ourselves and the audience. During a very emotional scene between the hero and heroine the other male members of the cast and myself were changing costumes, I heard a tittering break out in the audience. It developed into a roar.
>
> "Something was amiss. The scene was not supposed to be funny. Then I noticed by companion. He was between the light and the sheet and the audience was getting a first class view of a man in his shirt tail, hat on head, struggling into his trousers."[4]

Such incidents for the most part, were the rule, rather than the exception. A story is told about a company that rolled into a non-descript Eastern Ontario town only to discover the hall, in which it was to play, was situated next to the local jail. Space in the "theatre" was at a premium and, seeing that both cells were unoccupied, male members of the troupe were forced into the unique situation of dressing for the evening's performance – in jail.

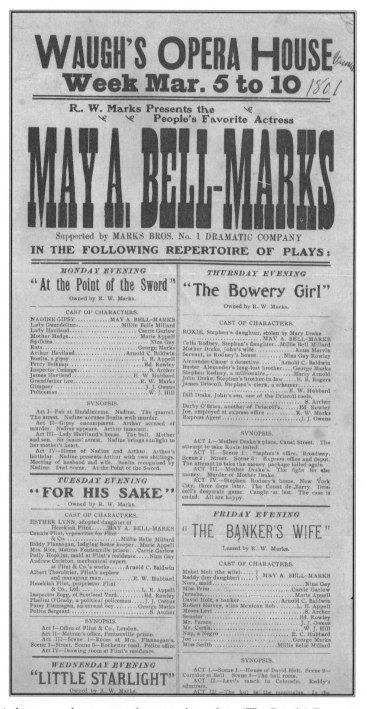

R.W. Marks was not hesitant in advertising his wife as "The People's Favourite Actress" as shown in this playbill. May A. Bell's versatility is demonstrated in this range of theatrical offerings.
Perth Museum Collection.

On another occasion, a wandering band of actors playing one-night stands found themselves in a hall that provided dressing facilities in the wings which had been designated for women only. The men were relegated to centre stage where they slapped on make-up clad only in their underclothes when someone tugged on the curtain cord. Before the howls of a packed house, they ducked for cover.

In most instances house props also left much to be desired. Stories abound about players having to use a crude kitchen chair covered with velveteen to give the appearance of luxurious furniture, while the actress, playing the role of a millionaire's wife with aid of a vivid imagination, fingered her five and dime pearls. May Bell Marks recalled an incident, when playing a woman of wealth, she summoned her servant and said, "Lights" only to have what few lights there were in the theatre go out.

On still another occasion, her improvisational talents were taxed to the hilt when a young stagehand, who became so engrossed with the performance, failed to drop the curtain on cue. When he did so, it dropped with such force that it actually bounced a foot off the floor.

> "A survival of days gone by is the apparatus for operating the curtain in certain village theatres. Some ten feet from the floor is a platform holding a large wheel which works the heavy screen. Here sits the operator throughout the performance, raising and lowering the curtain when a bell signals from below. It is from this quaint device we get the expression 'ring down the curtain.'"[5]

In January 1900, Gracie Whitcher, who had left the Marks Brothers to join her father's company, had returned to the fold following an incident the previous month which left her father's touring troupe stranded in Northern Ontario. On February 15, R.W. and Tom combined their companies to perform "East Lynne" and "The Major's Bride" before a capacity crowd of 2,700 in London, Ontario, possibly at the forerunner to London's Grand Theatre, which opened in 1901.

The Marks Brothers were now a household word. With this notoriety came the inevitable product endorsements:

> "No more successful company, and deservedly so, is on the road today than the Marks Brothers Company. Wherever they go, crowded houses greet them night after night and they are always welcome back. Merit tells. Exposed as they are to all kinds of weather travelling from place to place, they are liable to take cold, and their experience in the way of the

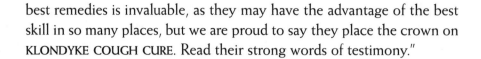

best remedies is invaluable, as they may have the advantage of the best skill in so many places, but we are proud to say they place the crown on KLONDYKE COUGH CURE. Read their strong words of testimony."

However, the company which placed this advertisement in the *Perth Expositor* of March 29, 1900, failed to include the Marks Brothers' words of endorsement. The promotion only appeared once, indicating it was probably printed without R.W.'s knowledge or consent.

From September 1899 to May 1900, the combined company concentrated its efforts in Michigan and southwestern Ontario, with the occasional jaunt into Hamilton and London. These engagements were followed by a seven-day booking in Brockville and Cornwall, where the brothers showed motion pictures in conjunction with the usual vaudeville routines.

On May 14, the company arrived at Christie Lake minus May Bell Marks and Georgie, who had gone to Brooklyn to visit family and friends. R.W. accompanied the pair to New York City, where he spent most of the time securing new plays and personnel for the forthcoming season. Tom and Joe also chose to begin their off-season activities in the "Big Apple." While in New York, Joe, always anxious to keep abreast of worldly events, had the opportunity to spend a great deal of time with members of the Boer delegation who were in the city to lobby support for the on-going Boer War in South Africa. In the meantime, Ernie, who chose to stay closer to home, accepted a private booking in Cornwall, where he performed on his trick wheel, "The Brantford Red Bird" and recited his "Uncle Josh" routine.

On June 15, Tom left the lake for Port Huron, Michigan, a new addition to the circuit. Three days later he was joined by Ernie. The summer would not be complete without playing an annual benefit for St. Stephen's Anglican Church. Even though Tom and Ernie were in Michigan and R.W. in Alexandria Bay, New York, making arrangements for rehearsal space before opening the 1900-1901 season in Perth on August 8, the company was well represented at the benefit by May Bell Marks, Millie Bell, Georgie and Joe Marks. A similar concert was held in Maberly, on August 3, this time under the auspices of St. Alban's Church.

On August 8, R.W.'s eighteen-member company opened a week's engagement at the Perth Opera House on D'Arcy Street. This facility, much smaller than the town hall, was located on the second floor above a dentist's office.

"The opening night of this season's engagement of the Marks Brothers Dramatic Company, was the occasion for the assemblying in the Opera

Mabel and Anna Purdue presenting a Scottish Reel during the 1899 to 1901 season.
Mabel Gracie Marintha Andrews, Joe's leading lady, used the stage name of Mabel Purdue for a number
of years. In 1905, at the age of 24, she would become Mrs. Joe Marks. Soon afterward she dropped her
first name and became well-known as Gracie Marks, "a star in her own right." *Courtesy Doug Bell.*

House here of the largest crowd ever seen in the hall at an entertainment. The hall was packed from the front to the back seats, chairs were placed in the aisles and the crowd filled the hall landing back to the stairs, and all this notwithstanding the sweltering heat...

"...the specialties are no small part of the performance and they alone are worth more than the price of admission, the audience being treated to some good singing, dancing trick bicycle riding and capital novelty dancing by the nimble-toed soubrettes. The moving pictures used in the illustrated songs were the clearest and by far the best ever seen here. May A. Bell Marks made the hit of the evening when she sang, 'My Heart's Tonight in Texas'....["]6

The feature attraction opening night was "Alone In London," "East Lynne" was offered at the Saturday matinee followed by "Harvest of Sin" in the evening.

After the Perth booking, R.W. and company played Smiths Falls for a week before heading across the border to Alexandria Bay. Within two days the troupe returned to the Perth Opera House and on Wednesday performed the perennial favourite, "A Bird in a Gilded Cage," on Thursday it was "Paradise Regained," on Friday, "A Soldier's Sweetheart," with the Saturday matinee being "Sundered Hearts" and Saturday night featuring "A Soldier's Daughter." Included in the company on this swing were May A. Bell Marks, Georgie Marks, Millie Bell, Gracie Whitcher, Alice Kemp, W. A. Moriarty, J. C. Connelly, W. A. Clarke, F. L. Godding, C. C. Miller, Eddie Horan, Pauline Geary, O. M. Cotten, M. L. Brantingham and W. Cherry.

Two former members of R.W.'s company, who had since gone their own separate ways, were also making news in the autumn of

Tom Marks, the consummate comedian, took his own Marks Brothers Company on the road. *Perth Museum Collection.*

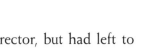

1900. W. E. Phillips, who had once been the troupe's stage director, but had left to manage the Théatre Français in Montreal, found himself in hot water when theatre owner, Daniel Ford, launched a $30,000 lawsuit against him for alleged carelessness in allowing the building to be burned to the ground.

James R. Field, it will be remembered, was one of the first American acts R.W. brought into Canada. At that time, the summer of 1893, he, along with his wife Gertrude and their two daughters, were billed as The Field's Mandolin Company, but they had since left the company and joined forces with a man called Mr. Devoe. Devoe was no stranger to the Marks brothers, as Tom had hired him in Michigan, when he was billed as Devoe and his "Wargraph." In 1899, the two men had formed their own company, and called themselves the Field and Devoe Company.

In early September, R.W. and his cohorts began an extensive tour of New York State, which ended at Jamestown in early January 1901. Then it was off to Erie, Pennsylvania, the first stop in a three month tour of the state, which concluded at Scranton on the 9th of March.

Three days later, R. W. and selected company members arrived at Christie Lake for some well-deserved rest and relaxation. Meanwhile, Tom was playing an engagement in Kingston. Shortly after R.W. arrived in Perth, he announced that a third Marks Brothers' company, under the combined management of Joe and Alex would take to the road in August. In late March, Joe left for Kingston, to take control of Tom's company for the remainder of the season. The reason for this change of command is not readily known, but it could be attributed to Tom's failing health – he had been suffering severe sciatica attacks for several years.

Neither R.W. or Tom had played Perth since August of the previous year, and as a result, the townspeople had been subjected to a number of companies, whose entertainments left much to be desired. One troupe in particular left an indelible mark on the community:

> "It is a pity that an entertainment having so many good points as the one given in the Town Hall on Friday night, 'Widow Brown,' should have been spoiled by the indelicate actions and jokes by the performers. The objectionable features might have been left out without affecting the run of the play, and then the funny parts would have been without alloy."[7]

In early June, Joe returned to Christie Lake, while Mack, the only brother still to don tophat and tails and take to the "boards," was busily engaged in pursuits that constituted a farmer's life. Tom, it would seem, preferred to go elsewhere after Joe took

May A. Bell Marks was the leading lady in her husband's company for many years. She is reputed to have had a repertoire of some 300 stage roles. *Perth Museum Collection.*

over command of his company. In all probability, he went either to Mount Clemens, Michigan or Hot Springs, Arkansas, in order to take solace in their soothing mineral waters. He returned to the lake the first week in July.

The success of the Marks Brothers' "theatrical empire" had not gone unnoticed in the industry. In June 1901, R.W. placed an advertisement in the trade publication, *New York Clipper*, soliciting additional talent to augment his company. By mid-July, following two special mail deliveries to the lake, he received over two hundred applications requesting employment.

While R.W. waded through this myriad of correspondence, Ernie, then twenty-two years old, was in Brockville, preparing for an event that would ultimately turn fact into fiction as far as his stage career was concerned. No longer would he be, in real life, the suave and dapper eligible bachelor that he portrayed in the theatre. His official role playing in this capacity came to an end on August 7, 1901, when he married sixteen-year-old, Katherine (Kitty) Reynolds of Brockville.

The wedding took place at the parsonage of St. Francis Xavier Church, and was presided over by the Reverend St. Amaud. Daisy Dugan, Kitty's childhood friend, acted as bridesmaid, while brother Edward gave away the bride. Joe stood as Ernie's best-man. Following the ceremony the newlyweds were greeted outside the church by a throng of well-wishers.

Ernie first met his prospective bride in 1900, while playing in Brockville. Their daughter, Bettie (Marks) Kelly, tells of the meeting:

> "Kitty was only fifteen-years-old and still going to school when she first laid eyes on Ernie. On her way to and from school, she would pass the hotel were the Marks Company was staying. One day she noticed the brothers standing in front of their lodgings, dressed elegantly in high silk hats and broad neckties. One of the boys, Ernie, who at that time was very slim and handsome, caught her attention.
>
> "For the next several days they carried on what can best be described as 'visual' courting – they would glance at each other and then turn their heads. On another occasion, while walking with her sister, Ethel, Kitty once again caught the attention of young Ernie; but as usual she continued on her way. However, Ethel, allowing her curiosity to get the better of her, turned and glanced at the brothers, she whispered to Kitty: 'Kitty! that tall, good-looking man, one of the Marks brothers is following us.'
>
> 'C'mon Ethel,' gasped Kitty, 'if mother knew that she'd skin me alive.'

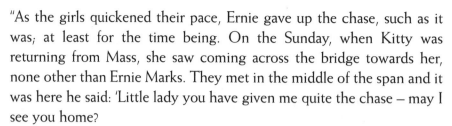

"As the girls quickened their pace, Ernie gave up the chase, such as it was; at least for the time being. On the Sunday, when Kitty was returning from Mass, she saw coming across the bridge towards her, none other than Ernie Marks. They met in the middle of the span and it was here he said: 'Little lady you have given me quite the chase – may I see you home?

"Of course, she answered yes. Having arrived at Kitty's residence, her mother rushed to the door anxious to discover why her daughter was alone in the company of a young man. Ernie, in his inimitable fashion , turned on the charm, so much indeed that he was invited to tea later in the afternoon. As the clock struck the appointed hour, Ernie could be seen driving down the street in a handsome rig, drawn by an equally handsome steed.

"When he arrived at the house, Ernie directed his attentions to Kitty's mother, suggesting she join him in a tour of Brockville. He also suggested that perhaps Ethel and Kitty might like to accompany them. That's how they met."

Ernie, due to the nature of his profession, was continually on the road, so a long distance love affair was carried on by correspondence until the summer of 1901, when he returned to Brockville and asked Kitty's mother for permission to marry her daughter.

But, there was one stumbling block to this otherwise fairy tale romance. Kitty was raised a Roman Catholic, while Ernie was a staunch Orangeman. As wedding plans were being discussed, it became evident that Kitty would not marry outside her church, and Ernie had no intention of converting to Catholicism. In order to circumvent this obstacle the couple decided to marry in the parsonage.

"I never heard my mother and father have one word of dissension about religion," remarked their daughter, Mrs. Bettie Kelly. "Every Sunday morning my mother would take myself and my three brothers to Mass, and when we came home that finished religion for the day. We never talked about it (religion) and we never tried to convert him to the Roman Catholic Church. "He lived his religion, by being a fine, solid and respectable man. He contributed financially, not only to the Catholic Church, but also to the United and Anglican faiths as well."

While Ernie and Kitty were enjoying their one week honeymoon, the rehearsal hall at Christie Lake was humming with activity as preparations for the forthcoming season were being finalized. Several personnel changes had also been made. Frederick H. Wilson, formerly a comedian and dance man was elevated to the position of stage director with R.W.'s company. Carl Bayard Steers, of St. Louis, Missouri, became stage director for Joe's troupe.

On August 1, 1901, Ella Marks and her daughter, Arlie, returned to the lake from London, about the same time as the R.W. and May Bell Marks were also at the lake celebrating the birth and subsequent baptism of their first child, a daughter, May Marguerite (Maizie). In keeping with tradition, the Marks Brothers continued to play benefit concerts for the local church. This time the sole recipient of the proceeds from the entertainment, given August 2 at the Burton homestead near Maberly, was Reverend C.E.S. Radcliffe. The Reverend had fallen victim to financial hardships as a result of an extended convalescence at Kingston Hospital. As usual, the event was well attended and netted the ailing cleric $99.45. Members from R.W.'s, Tom's and Joe's companies, including Fred Miller who whistled his way through several encores after regaling his audience with comic dialogues, volunteered their services. Tom and his daughter, Arlie, combined their singing talents, while Ernie and Chris Allen doubled up for an Irish skit. Kitty Marks,

Gracie, the headliner in Joe Mark's company, shown in her role as Jerry in "The Parson's Nephew," during the 1901-1902 theatrical season. *Perth Museum Collection.*

who had now taken to the stage along with her husband, joined May A. Bell Marks and Fanny Brombridge in several songs. Arnold C. Baldwin, leading man in R.W.'s company, teamed up with Jack Connelly, Alice Kemp-Brantingham and Claude Miller to perform

Joe Marks, at the time the manager of the Marks Brothers A-1
Company. On the back, Gracie has written "My much loved Joe."
Courtesy Doug Bell.

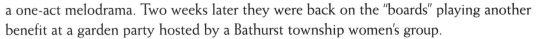

a one-act melodrama. Two weeks later they were back on the "boards" playing another benefit at a garden party hosted by a Bathurst township women's group.

On Thursday, August 23, the 1901-02 touring season officially got underway when Alex's and Joe's company began a two day engagement at the Perth Opera House. As the curtain dropped on the Saturday performance of "Hazel Kirk," the troupe was asked to play two additional dates, August 28 and August 30. The Wednesday night performance (August 28) was a benefit for the (Perth) Crescent Lacrosse Club. On this occasion, John A. Stevens' play, "Passion's Slave" was presented, and on Friday, Frank Tannerhill's play, which was originally made famous by Lizzie Evans, "Mugs Landing'" was the evening's fare.

Capitalizing on the overwhelming success of this troupe, the management of the Perth Opera House once again offered Alex and Joe additional dates, which lasted until September 11. During this engagement the company presented several plays including "The Black Flag" "East Lynne," "Forgiven," "Camille," "The Two Orphans," and "Under Two Flags," – all for the low price of ten cents for general admission and fifteen cents for reserved seats.

During the two week Perth engagement Joe's company was augmented with the talents of R.W. and May A. Bell Marks, along with Ernie and Kitty. After leaving Perth, the company travelled north to play the towns of Pembroke and Arnprior, before returning for entertainments in Carleton Place and Smiths Falls. The troupe then left for an extended tour of the United States, which lasted until late March 1902.

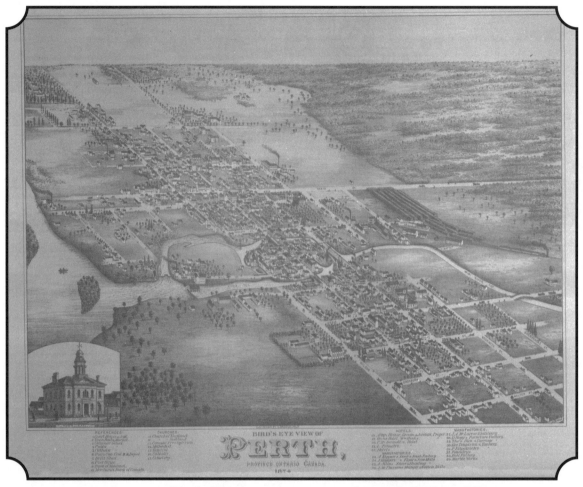

A representation of Perth, Ontario, circa 1874, artist unknown. *Perth Museum Collection*.

CHAPTER 8

PERILS OF THE STAGE – BUT THE SHOW MUST GO ON

By March 30, 1902, the brothers, with the exception of R.W., had returned to the lake to indulge in another of their favourite recreational activities – baseball. On this particular occasion several troupe members including Tom, Ernie and Alex challenged a team of Perth town officials and businessmen – and won.

The love of baseball and other sporting activities played a prominent role in the lives of the Marks family for many years. For instance, in 1929 the Christie Lake Bearcats softball team was formed, and continued to play, albeit, under different names until 1946. Ernie's sons, Jack, Joe and Ted, along with Joe Perkins, Law Sheppard, Grant Garrette, Allan James, Art Cross, Donnie Brown, Red and Eddie Conway, were the first players on the team, and several of them continued to play into the 1940s.

While Tom, Alex and Ernie were playing baseball, R.W. and company were in the process of wrapping-up the season, and arrived at the lake in mid-April. Following a few days rest the companies combined once again and gave a performance at the Maberly Town Hall. Following the concert, R.W. began rehearsals for a spring tour which would take the troupe through Eastern Ontario and a two week jaunt through Quebec.

On May 2, the fifteen-member company opened in Perth with "Camille." "The Crimes of London" was presented at the Saturday matinee and the two-day stand closed with "The Innkeeper's Daughter." Early Sunday morning the troupe caught a train for a two week stint in Almonte. R.W. and his cohorts continued to play the towns and villages of Eastern Ontario until late May, when he joined Joe's and Alex's company in Cornwall. When the season finally closed on June 7, Robert W. Marks' troupe had been on the road for thirty-six weeks.

Ernie, who was still touring with Joe and Alex, was gaining a reputation as a first-class comedian, as was his wife, Kitty, for her singing and dancing. But during the latter part of the year, Kitty took a leave of absence from the company in order to have her baby, which was born at Brockville on May 26. Unfortunately, however, the infant, christened Joseph Ernest, died of complications on October 27.

After leaving Cornwall the companies made their way to Christie Lake, where the usual regimen of creating new scenery, rehearsing plays and refining musical routines got underway. But, it was not all work. Joe, Alex and Mack, in keeping with their tradition of celebrating the "Glorious Twelfth," went to Brockville to take in the celebrations. At the same time, Tom was packing trunks, props and scenery for his company's opening at Kalamazoo, Michigan, in late August. A month later he was joined by Chris Allen and other members of the cast.

In mid-August, Alex, Ernie and Joe, accompanied by Lydia Poe, left Perth for a week's "paid" rehearsals at Prescott. On August 25, R.W.'s company began similar rehearsals at Perth, in preparation for performances on August 27 and 30.

After leaving Perth, R.W. took the company to Ogdensburg, New York, and the entertainment void was filled by one of the several circuses that regularly travelled throughout the region. It would seem, however, this form of diversion had found little favour with some townspeople, including the editor of the *Perth Courier*:

> "Don't take too much money with you to the circus; and what you do take, don't risk it on any fake games. Give the children a good chance to see the animals, explaining as much as possible to them. Don't be afraid to drink too much lemonade, unless you object to water in great quantities. Be sure to give the children enough money to see the parade and the exhibitions outside the grounds. Don't meddle with the monkeys; they bite deep."[1]

R.W. opened at Ogdensburg on September 4, with the five-act melodrama "Lost In London." Crowded houses were the order of the day during the six-day engagement. On more than one occasion May Bell Marks was the recipient of numerous ovations for her dual role as Annie Meadows and Nan, the flower girl. Plaudits were also heaped upon Jack C. Connelly and villain, Will T. Stewart, who received more than a liberal share of hisses and jeers. On closing night the company boarded a train for other locales in northern New York State, before heading for a two-week booking in Pembroke, followed by a one week's return engagement at the Perth Opera House beginning September 29.

Both Scottish and Irish themes were frequently part of the Marks Brothers repertoire.
This later photograph shows Tom Marks and His Kilties prior to their performance at the Rideau
Theatre. Seated front right is Jim Perrin, Tom's son-in-law. *Courtesy Doug Bell.*

While in Perth, R.W., never missing an opportunity to demonstrate his latent talent as a comedian, wrote to a Scottish outfitter in Arnprior inquiring as the availability of acquiring a kilt and accompanying apparel which were needed to bolster the troupe's wardrobe collection. In his letter, R.W. implied that he didn't know the generic term for a sporran, so he referred to it as something resembling a brush for whitewashing.

While R.W. and company were in Perth, Tom was still trooping through Michigan. During a booking in Ann Arbour, he and several male members of the cast created such an impact on several members of the audience that they were inducted into the local chapter of the Elk's Lodge.

Even as love blossomed on the stage, which of course, was the basic theme of most melodramas, so it did off stage. In late November, May Bell Marks' younger sister, Millie, announced, while playing at Governeur, New York, her forthcoming marriage to fellow actor, W.C. Millard. This was not the only surprise in store for R.W. On December 8, at a theatre in Rome, New York, Jack Connelly fell through a trap door and fractured his collar bone. Connelly's unfortunate accident was by no means an isolated incident. Over the years a number of actors, actresses and stage hands had fallen victim to the "perils of the stage."

All too often, players, especially those engaged in one-night stands and who were unfamiliar with their new surroundings, were often required to make hurried changes in their routines because of unforeseen hazards. Such was the case when a troupe performed in one small Ontario town. The evening's performance required three entrances, two sides and one centre. Because of space limitations, players had to do without the centre exit, although most exits in the production were made from this strategic point. Not having rehearsed this change, the performers were kept constantly on their toes so as not to run into each other.

On still another occasion, the stage floor sloped towards the footlights at a such a perilous angle that players deemed it a hazard to both life and limb. It was only by sheer will power that no one suffered the ignominy of falling into the front row seats. A loose carpet covering a slippery floor was the culprit on still another stage. During an emotional scene between the leading man and woman, a third party was to make an entrance bringing important news. As he stepped from the wings onto the carpet, he slipped, sending his legs and arms flailing in every direction. It was only through a series of violent contortions that he managed to save himself from falling. Of course, the audience by this time was in a fit of hysterics.

On January 23, 1903, after completing his American tour, R.W., three days later, began a six-day run at the Grand Theatre in Ottawa. While in the capitol city, May Bell

The death scene of Cigarette, the heroine played by May. A Bell Marks in the popular play "Under Two Flags." *Perth Museum Collection.*

Marks and her sister received word their father had died in Brooklyn, New York, on January 23. The Ottawa booking was followed by three days in Carleton Place and nine days in Peterborough, which in turn was followed by performances in Lindsay and Orillia.

Tom was still touring through Michigan and southwestern Ontario at this time. During the week of March 16, he played St. Thomas after breaking the house record at Andrain, Michigan. By now, R.W. was "holding court" in Collingwood, before moving on to Owen Sound and London. In the latter locale, the sixteen-member company opened with a new variation on an old theme "Crimes In London." This play was no doubt a modification on the old standbys "Alone In London" and "Lost In London." Also, "A Soldier's Daughter" was presented and leading lady, May Bell Marks, besides participating in both melodramas, also sang several illustrated songs. W.C. Willard performed Dutch specialties, Rawley & Gay entertained with Scottish ditties, Frank Gregory juggled hoops and clubs, while young George Marks sang and danced his way through a number of encores.

When the company closed its season in mid-May, R.W. had been on the road for thirty-two weeks touring New York State and Ontario. As usual, the brothers returned to Christie Lake for the summer, and by September were back on the road again; but from then until mid-November the whereabouts of all three companies is unknown. That is, until November 19, when Mr. and Mrs. Thomas Marks Sr. celebrated their golden wedding anniversary. Throughout, the parents remained totally supportive of their sons' vocations. Any stroke of good fortune befalling one son or daughter became a matter of general family rejoicing. Regrettably, R.W. was the only son able to attend as Tom, Joe, Alex and Ernie were playing in St. Thomas.

From November to early April 1904, nothing is known of the comings and goings of the brothers, but we do know Mack Marks was still at the lake busily engaged in his favourite pastime – horse racing.

The *Daily Journal* of April 8, 1904, published at Montpelier, Vermont, reported R.W. and company played the Blanchard Opera House the night before and presented "Mabel Heath."

> "... May Bell Marks in her songs was thoroughly enjoyed and was compelled to repeated encores. Her song 'As Welcome as the Flowers in May' was especially good. Areno was in more of his wonderful contortionist acts. George Marks' play to the 'gallery gods' in his song 'Gallery Boys For Me,' won their hearts. Millard on the bicycle and Rawley & Gay in their skit were all excellent. The moving pictures formed a pleasing feature of the show."

R.W. closed the season at Burlington, Vermont on April 23, and reached Christie Lake on April 27. With the exception of a few bookings in Eastern Ontario, the company had played most of its engagements in New York State and Vermont. Joe, Alex and Ernie closed their season at Perth in June. Meanwhile, Tom announced he had secured the services of Laura Winston for the 1904-05 season. Previously, Winston had been the leading lady with Hoyt's Comedy Company. R.W. was also acquiring additional talent in the manner of Eddie Horan, whom he had spirited away from the Haverly's Minstrels. As well, Fred Cummings was appointed as the company's musical director.

In 1904, the theatrical industry as it pertained to Ontario and Quebec was undergoing dramatic changes, the first of which was the introduction of the Main Line Theatrical Circuit. This organization was similar in theory, but not in scope to Franklin Keith's and Edward F. Albee's American [Theatre] Circuit, with its base in New York City. These gentlemen used a combination of aggressiveness, shrewdness and a good deal of ruthlessness in building a vaudeville empire that was second to none. The Main

According to *The Billboard* article of November 19, 1921, written by Robson Black, May A. Bell Marks was "letter-perfect" in all of her extensive repertoire of "long parts" and "is ready to appear on two hours summons." *Perth Museum Collection*.

Line Circuit operated on the basis that it alone could ensure only the best attractions would be permitted to play in those theatres that chose to join its ranks. In its simplest form the Main Line was engaging in a minor, but perfectly legal form of extortion, having announced that unless the local theatre joined the consortium, it was highly unlikely any theatrical company would ever play there.

The circuit, it was said, embraced over thirty of the most important cities and towns in Ontario between Sarnia and Montreal. In order to join the compact, theatrical companies had to undergo an "ordeal by fire." The troupe's merits were tested by a panel of "expert" critics and should it fail the inquisition, the company was immediately dismissed. But if it passed, the troupe was at liberty to traverse the entire circuit at will.

The first "circuit" attraction to play Perth on May 14 was "The Heart of Texas" (company unknown). This was followed by "For Her Sake," Marks Brothers A-1 Company; "The Hot Air Merchant," "Thelma" and "The Runaway Girl," by the Bijou Comedy Company. The Thomas' Minstrels rendition of "Jerry From Kerry" was next on the bill followed by Tom Marks' Stock Company's "My Wife's Family." "Romeo and Juliet" was presented by the Sullivan's Minstrels; the Power's Stock Company entertained with "Uncle Tom's Cabin"; "The Little Outcast" was offered by Field's Minstrels and the Irene Jeavous Stock Company presented "Monte Cristo."

On May 28, the Marks Brothers A-1 Company, under Joe's management, wrapped up a three-day engagement at the Perth Opera House. For the price of admission, fifteen and twenty-five cents, theatre-goers were entertained with "Sin and Sorrow," "Tennessee Pardner," "The Trapper's Daughter" and "The Shadow Detective." At the Saturday matinee a new gimmick was introduced – give-aways. On this occasion, Miss Mary Beattie won a two-dollar pair of shoes. Joe closed the season on June 18 and returned to the lake.

Giveaways were not a common practice during the heyday of melodrama and vaudeville (1890s to early 1930s), but it did become a fact of life during the Depression Years when theatre managers found it difficult to attract audiences through the week. In order to combat this undesirable situation, one small-town showman devised a sensational scheme which he hoped would improve Monday-night attendance. On the chosen night he advertised that he would give away free – a baby. The publicity agent was charged with informing and agitating the police about the impending event. When officers barged into the theatre, they were met by the manager who explained there was nothing legally wrong with his plan, "the mother doesn't object" he said calmly. Needless to say the house was filled to capacity and the showman lived up to his promise – and gave away a baby pig.

A manager's life was not all wine and roses; take for instance the case of James Burns:

Tom Marks as one of his favourite comedic characters, "Jiggs," in "Bringing Up Father," based on the famous George McManus comic strip. The original photograph was taken by the Adams Studio of Perth, Ontario. *Perth Museum Collection*.

Tom Marks brought Jiggs to life on stage. Photographed by the Adams studio, Perth.
Perth Museum Collection

"James Burns, manager of the theatrical company playing 'Reuben In New York,' was brutally assaulted in Brockville on Wednesday (June 9) by James Grant and Jos. Kearney, two members of the troupe. The trouble began the night before during the performance at the Grand Opera House, when these two men demanded a week's salary in advance. On being refused they initiated a row behind the scenes, which two constables were called to quell. They left the building after the first act, thinking to break up the show, but it went on. Thursday morning they found Burns in the in the reading-room of his hotel and administered a sound thrashing. He was so badly battered about the head and face that a doctor was called. His assailants escaped on the ferry boat to New York before the police had an opportunity to place them under arrest. The incident resulted in the company disbanding."[2]

On a lighter note, R.W., May Bell Marks, Millie J. Marks (Ellen perhaps?) and Olivia Marks, returned to Perth on June 17 following a four-day excursion to the Thousand Islands and Montreal. During their stay in Montreal, R.W. left orders for scenery and wardrobe which would be used in his latest production, "Anona, The Indian Maid." By July 8, Ella Marks and daughter Arlie, who had been attending school in Oshawa, along with Kitty Marks and her infant son, Jack, also arrived at the lake. It is interesting to note the *Perth Courier* in this report of July 8, 1904, noted that Joe Marks was still a bachelor. But not for long – he would marry his leading lady in late 1905.

Several actors in the Marks' companies had now begun to make Christie Lake a regular vacation spot. It would seem R.W. no longer insisted that contract players return to the lake for rehearsals during the off season. But such was not the case with new personnel. Mr. and Mrs. Appell and a Mr. Burr, vaudeville acts from New York City, began their careers with the Marks Brothers by rehearsing at Christie Lake.

Land around the lake, at least for the Marks family, was available for the asking, on payment of a nominal sum to Thomas Sr. But Joe opted for an alternative; he purchased an island not far from the mainland and called it Joe's Island. After he married Gracie, the name was changed to Ruby Island. This picturesque piece of real estate, although nothing more than a barren outcrop of granite, supported minimal vegetation and even fewer trees. However, there was just enough land on which to build a small cottage with just enough room left over to make the property comfortable.

During the summer of 1904, while Joe was busily engaged in burning some accumulated leaves, he unearthed an old Indian fireplace which had been used by Indians and hunters some forty years previous. After further investigation Joe discovered the island had been the camping ground of an Indian named Stevens. On his hunting trips Stevens was usually accompanied by his wife along with two other men and their women. Adjacent to the fireplace he found a mound lying east and west, which he surmised was a burying ground.

During the summer of 1904, Tom did not return to the lake because of his theatrical commitments in and around Michigan. He finally closed the season August 20, at Sault. Ste. Marie, Michigan, and then moved across the border to the Canadian "Soo," where he spent a week reorganizing the company which now boasted twelve new faces. The following week he opened a six day engagement at the "Soo" opera house.

Immediately following the Perth booking, R.W. and company headed for the border and began touring New York State and Vermont. The *Ogdensburg News* of September 20, 1904, reported the troupe, had played there September 16, 17 and 19, and had taken the town by storm with three record-breaking nights to their credit. In the meantime, Joe's company had played five nights in Kingston with equal success. That same week the *Winnipeg Telegram* announced Tom and his company had arrived in the city. It also said he had broken the "hoodoo" that was supposedly attached to the Auditorium Theatre by drawing bumper houses at each performance.

The death of Thomas Marks Sr., of an apoplectic stroke on October 16, came as a great surprise to family and friends. He was, for all intents and purposes, a robust individual, who continued to work up until his death. Joe, Alex and Ernie cut short a booking in St. Catharines, as did R.W. who travelled from Montpelier, Vermont, to attend the funeral. Tom was unable to attend as he was playing in Brandon, Manitoba.

A barely discernable Joe (left) in his canoe. From the Joe and Gracie Marks album. *Courtesy of Doug Bell.*

Joe Marks relaxing at his beloved Ruby Island. Once retired, he and Gracie became residents at the lake, until his death in 1944. From the Joe and Gracie Marks album.
Courtesy of Doug Bell.

Maizie, daughter of May A. Bell and R.W., at five years of age. She joined her mother on the stage, at a very early age. *Courtesy Elton Crandall.*

This photograph of a three-year-old Robert J. Marks was chosen as the "Most Beautiful Child" in the *Toronto Sunday World* photo contest about 1914. He became a boy comedian and had aspirations for a career on the stage, only to find that by adulthood the days of the travelling theatrical shows were on their way out. *Perth Museum Collection.*

CHAPTER 9

HONING TALENT OVER THE YEARS

The year 1905 finally brought news of John Jay Marks, the first since 1895 when he had left Christie Lake for the Dakotas. He was now residing in British Columbia, and through a combination of hard work and good luck, had become successful in the mining industry, owning three mines in the area surrounding Hedley. But during the week of January 9 to 14 he took time off from his hectic schedule and visited his brother, Tom, who was playing in nearby Nelson.

In February, Tom left the West Coast, and trooped through the villages and towns of the Northwest Territories. At Prince Albert (now part of Saskatchewan) he met a former Perth resident, Corporal J. W. Spalding, of the North West Mounted Police. Spalding would go on to have an illustrious career with the "redcoats" that culminated with him being appointed Deputy Commissioner of the Royal Canadian Mounted Police before his retirement. However, their first meeting proved to be less than an auspicious occasion.

While sitting in the Prince Albert Hotel, Tom was accidentally shot in the foot by a .22 calibre revolver that Spalding was carrying in his pocket. A few hours earlier he had taken the gun from a drunken reveller. Luckily, the bullet glanced off an eyelet in Tom's shoe and penetrated only a few inches into his foot.

While Tom was busily engaged playing his impromptu game of "cowboys and Indians" and touring other western cities and towns, R.W. continued his jaunt through the northern United States and Ontario. Meanwhile, Joe preferred Michigan, all their touring routes having been carefully arranged in advance. In June, Carl B. Steers, who had toured with both R.W.'s and Tom's companies, ended his theatrical career to start a

Gracie Marks perfected her "little girl" roles, way beyond her arrival into adulthood. This photo, undated, was dedicated "To Papa." On the back of the photo, she described her elaborate costume: white organdy over red, with ruffled silk-edged pleated underskirts, red velvet ribbon trimmings and red silk hose and red slippers. *Perth Museum Collection*.

On the back of this 1906 studio still taken by Gillespie & Co. of North Bay, someone (name not decipherable) had written to Gracie saying that this was "the nicest *soubrette* photograph he had ever seen." *Perth Museum Collection*.

In her later years, under her own name as the May A. Bell Company, May Bell Marks mounted children's extravaganzas. A review dated December 27, 1923, described the Toronto production of "The Sleeping Beauty" as being costumed and staged "in a faultless manner" and "proved a source of keen enjoyment to immense audiences." *Perth Museum Collection.*

newspaper in Patterson, Tennessee. Steers was not the only actor to leave the fold at this time; C.W. Otis, who had been Tom's advance agent, left for a similar position with Lemon Brothers' Circus.

Two months later, R.W. made another announcement that a fourth Marks Brothers' company, under the combined management of Ernie and Mack, would take to the road by the end of the year.

During August and September, R.W. and his company played the Eastern Ontario towns of Perth, Smiths Falls, Arnprior and Pembroke. Here theatre-goers were treated to such melodramatic gems as "Canada," "An Alabama Home," "Jane The Westerner," "My Tennessee Partner," "The Whirlwind Harvest" and "Dr. Jekyll and Mr. Hyde."

After leaving Michigan, Joe and company headed to Northern Ontario, and "held the boards" at Sturgeon Falls before moving on to Sudbury. In late October, Ernie was playing Oshawa:

"Ernie Marks is without a doubt the best Marks Brothers' Company that has visited Oshawa."[1]

On November 9, 1905, Mack Marks finally took the plunge and left Perth for Guelph, where he would join Ernie and Joe. Prior to leaving the homestead, Mack had sold off all his livestock and farm implements, and moved his mother and two sisters into Perth for the winter.

Special Children's Matinee Saturday Afternoon January 5th, 2 P.M.
MAY-BELL MARKS AND COMPANY
IN
JACK AND THE BEANSTALK
Admission for the Kiddies to the Matinee, 10 Cents, Including Tax

By Special Request
Commencing, Monday Jan. 7th.
(For One Week Only)
May-Bell Marks and Co. Will Present
Little Red Riding Hood
IN THREE ACTS AND SIX SCENES
The Popular Fairy Tale—The Kiddies Will Love to See

WILLIAM FOX presents
Dustin Farnum
KENTUCKY DAYS
story by JOHN LYNCH directed by DAVID SOLOMON

Announcing MAY-BELL MARKS CO., in a Grand Pan
"The Sleeping Beaut"
Commencing Christmas Day Matinee at 2.15   Limited Engagemen

Often these publicity stills were autographed and sent to friends and fans. This one, also taken by Gillespie & Co., was sent to a lady in St. Thomas in 1908. Here Gracie describes her gown as mauve with a white silk edge and a European spangled tunic. On the front of one of her many photos, Gracie has written, "Feeling old, trying to look young ...." *Perth Museum Collection*.

After leaving Pembroke, R.W. crossed the border into Portland, Maine. They opened at the Jefferson Theatre with "Little Starlight," with May A. Bell Marks in the leading role. The production also featured five-year-old Maizie Marks, who wowed the audience with her illustrated songs. R.W., in his interview for *The Billboard* in 1921 commented on the children travelling with their companies. While he recognized their publicity value – "children are great business-getters especially at matinees" – he noted the need to limit their time on stage or risk the indignation of mothers. For the children it was superb training for future roles.

Tom Marks, famous for his Irish brogue comedic sketches, prominently displays his "famous" three-stone diamond ring. As he was known to have said, "... safest place, on the finger." This publicity still is dated circa 1920. *Perth Museum Collection*.

In early December, Joe's and Alex's company, along with the new company, managed by Ernie and Mack, were in Western Ontario. Now that the Marks Brothers had become a household name, community newspapers across the province reported that Joe's leading lady, Gracie Andrews, had become his bride.

Gracie (Andrews) Marks, who was christened, Mabel Grace Marintha Andrews, was born at Grand Rapids, Michigan, in 1881. Nothing is known of her ancestry or formative years, but when she joined Joe's company (date unknown) she used the stage name Mabel Purdue. However, shortly after their marriage Gracie was forced to drop her first name, Mabel, and use her middle name. It is reported that May A. Bell Marks could not tolerate the idea of her name being confused with that of Mabel Marks.

Joe's leading man at this time was H. Webb Chamberlain, who, in later years would form his own company thanks to the experience he gained while with the Marks Brothers.

From December 11-16, 1905, Joe and Alex were booked to play the Guelph Fat Stock Fair which, according to the local newspaper, was considered one of the biggest dates in Western Ontario for any itinerant company. At the same time, brothers, Ernie and Mack were playing Stratford. In mid-November, Gracie Marks had left the company to be with her terminally ill mother in Grand Rapids. She returned to pick up the company in Guelph after the funeral on November 25.

Mack, it would seem was the only brother able to celebrate Christmas with his parents. He arrived in Perth a few days before the event, and left for Oshawa on January 2, 1906. In mid-January, John Jay Marks was in the news again, this time it was in the form of a wedding announcement. On January 17, he had married Blanche Brown of Hedley, British Columbia. It is not known for certain, but it is believed that Blanche Brown (b. 1884) was a one-time leading lady in the short-lived Theatre Royal Company of Victoria.

During their years on the road, the Marks Brothers came into contact with many touring companies, including the Guy Brothers' Minstrels, who were well-known to Ontario theatre-goers. On February 26, 1906, W.H. Guy, eldest brother of the minstrel troupe, passed away at his Springfield, Ohio, home. Guy was one of the oldtimers of the industry, and extremely dedicated to his profession. During his last performance at Perth in 1903, he was totally blind but still performed admirably.

Ernie and Mack, who were now affiliated with the Main Line Theatre Circuit, played Perth between March 1and 3, where they presented "Old Kentucky" and their new melodrama, "Louis Riel," along with eight vaudeville and specialty acts. Joe and Alex were also busy "plying their trade" during January and February, having played Kingston, Brockville, Belleville, Orillia and Lindsay. However, in late February, Alex was back in Perth recuperating from injuries suffered in a fall at St. Thomas.

On March 12, R.W. and company began a two-week booking at the Grand Theatre in Ottawa. Five days later, on St. Patrick's Day, Tom, who had returned from his western swing, presented the Irish comedy, "Shamus O' Byrne," in Smiths Falls. Two days later, Tom opened a three-day engagement in Perth with "The Irish Boarder," and a moving picture entitled "The Faithful Dog." Three of his major attractions during this booking were Chris Allen, Irma Leham and the Musical Archers. On Tuesday, March 20, he presented one of

Arlie Marks, *soubrette*, daughter of Tom and Ella Marks, with her "acting" dog, Patsy, circa 1914.
Perth Museum Collection.

his own plays, "A Soldier Of France," followed by "Shamus O' Byrne" on Wednesday. The proceeds from the Wednesday matinee were donated to the Perth Hockey Club, and the remainder of the week was played in Smiths Falls before swinging to Western Ontario.

The theatrical tradition of Tom and Ella Marks was, not surprisingly, inherited by their youngest daughter, Arlie. At a very early age she proved a quick study, touring with her parents and other experienced performers. She was often seen in early stage appearances with pet "Patsey," a bull terrier much at home in the footlights. One of Arlie's most endearing performances was her coveted role in the show "Peg O' My Heart."

Throughout this period, Ernie and Joe Marks regularly combined live performances and early moving pictures projected by a kinetescope. Because of their efforts "The Great Train Robbery" was shown between acts two and three of "The Orphans." At one point a newspaper clipping reported this film reel as having been stolen in Guelph. Gracie noted in her album that it cost Joe $150.00 to replace it. Both of the brothers were known for their innovative approaches to family entertainment, often putting on a trick cyclist between acts one and two of "East Lynne." Ernie and Joe, as was the case with all seven brothers, were businessmen first and showmen second. They knew the importance of providing a full evening's entertainment.

Each of the brothers took it hard when their father, Thomas Senior, passed away on October 16, 1904. Fortunately, they were to have the mother they all respected and

Arliedale, the Marks homestead, by now the home of Tom and Ella Marks, was operated as an inn during their retirement years. *Perth Museum Collection.*

Mother (Margaret Farrell) Marks on Ruby Island, home of Joe and Gracie Marks. *The Billboard* article of 1921 refers to her as being far past 80 years of age but "still in vigor of body and mind, to whom the children rally once a year as to their common friend and leader." She passed away later that year, mourned by all. *Courtesy Elton Crandall.*

adored until 1921, when she too passed on. Gone forever with the loss of Thomas and Margaret was the closeness to pioneer times those left behind had once known through their homesteading parents.

Though much of their time was spent on the road, each brother and their families enjoyed time spent at Christie Lake. Fishing parties, canoeing and cruises on the yacht *Maizie* provided precious hours of relaxation for family and visitors. The yacht, named after the little daughter of Robert W. and May Bell Marks, was a trim white vessel powered by coal oil. Actors and actresses rehearsing at the lake frequently made up the passengers aboard.

Joe and Ernie Marks had more in common than their name and a penchant for experimentation with their shows. Both brothers were married to their leading ladies. Katherine (Kitty) Reynolds had many good years touring as the leading lady in husband Ernie's stock company. A talented singer and comedienne, she is reported to have been the first female performer to play the Balderson Theatre located on Perth's Gore Street, often described as the finest theatre between Toronto and Montreal.

Kitty and Ernie Marks closed their company around 1922 and moved to Oshawa, where they bought the old movie house, which later became known as the Marks Theatre. Ernie went on to become one of the most popular mayors to ever hold the office of Oshawa's chief magistrate. He remained active in the "Motor City" until his death in 1952. The widowed Kitty lived on in Oshawa until her passing in 1962.

Possibly the most debonaire of all the brothers, Joseph also had more formal education than his siblings. Reports have it that his theological studies came to a halt suddenly, six months before his ordination as a clergyman. Opinions differ as to whether it was the lure of the stage or a romance that altered for all time his life. But the ministry's loss proved to be a big win for Canada's entertainment scene.

Hardworking, imaginative and totally conscientious, he possessed all the ingredients necessary for success in the demanding world of show business. But Joe was

An advertisement for the Ernie Marks Stock Co. *Perth Museum Collection.*

The interior of the Balderson Theatre in Perth had an opera house decor, with two floors, including a balcony that could seat about 700 patrons. The Marks troupes would have performed frequently, performed here. For a period of time, it was owned by the Premier Operating Corporation of Toronto. *Perth Museum Collection.*

Kitty Marks, in 1958, remembers her days as a star in her husband's theatrical troupe.
On the wall, over her right shoulder, is a portrait of Kitty at 23 years of age.
Taken from a *Maclean's* article of June 21, 1958. *Perth Museum Collection.*

also destined for a rewarding life on the personal level thanks to his leading lady, Mabel Purdue (Andrews), soon known as Gracie Marks. An attentive, loving wife, Mrs. Marks in time became a theatrical star of considerable stature, a skilled comedienne and an especially talented child impersonator.

In their day, Joe and Gracie lived a long, enjoyable life at Christie Lake, and were closely identified with such local landmarks as Ruby Island and Joe's Point. Joe's canoe and Gracie's rowing skiff would today be valuable collectibles, but they too are part of a vanished era.

Kitty and Ernie Marks on the occasion of their 50th Wedding Anniversary, 1951.
Their children were present for the family celebrations. The photograph was taken by the
Hornsby Studio of Oshawa. *Perth Museum Collection*.

Joe Marks, after retiring from his own theatrical company, kept his hand in the business by becoming a 50-50 partner with a famous Canadian magician. He would manage Bert Johnston's company for two seasons, from 1927 to 1928. *Perth Museum Collection*.

An advertising flyer, circa 1927. *Perth Museum Collection.*

George Whitman Marks, the actor, son of May A. Bell. This photograph was taken at the Hopkins Studio of St. Thomas, Ontario, date unknown. *Perth Museum Collection*.

CHAPTER 10

THE END OF AN ERA

Well over 75 years have passed since the last of the Marks Brothers shows came off the road. One by one, the brothers retired from show business, in several cases returning to their original roots at Christie Lake. Those were the days when they and their offspring owned 16 cottages around the lake. The very same locale that for years on end was the site of their working holidays, as the operators and members of the various companies mapped out tours, learned new scripts, refurbished sets and created new wardrobes.

If there is a shrine to their memory, it is the same sparking Christie Lake that their Irish homesteader grandfather had termed "The Killarney of Canada."

The family plot in the Elmwood Cemetery became the final resting place for a number of the brothers, their wives and offspring. May Bell Marks died at the Toronto General Hospital in 1932 in her 61st year. A sudden illness leading to her death interrupted negotiations with Toronto and Montreal interests to produce a series of radio plays. George Whitman Marks, May Bell's son from her first marriage, died in 1955.

Tom Marks died in 1935 at 81 years of age, his extraordinary sense of humour intact to the final curtain. Tom's wife, Ella, predeceased him in 1931. Their talented daughter, Arlie (after whom Arliedale Inn was named), died in Chicago, Illinois in 1941. Her husband and fellow performer, Jim Perrin, passed away in 1959.

Big brother Bob (R.W.) expired in 1937 at the age of 84. Notices of his death appeared coast to coast in Canada and the U.S.A. At the time of his passing, following a lengthy illness, R.W. was acknowledged by the media to be Canada's oldest theatrical producer. At one time, Robert W. and his brothers owned most of Christie Lake and

A representation of the Arliedale Inn, the old Marks homestead, as shown in a newspaper article on the Marks Brothers, published by the *Perth Courier* on August 22, 1963. *Perth Museum Collection*.

MONTREAL 149 Miles   TORONTO 188 Miles   KINGSTON   55 Miles   OTTAWA 55 Miles   BROCKVILLE 47 Miles

RED CEDAR INN

R. J. MARKS, Manager

Standard Hotel, on main line of the Canadian Pacific railway and connecting with the new Madoc to Ottawa Highway. 12 passenger trains daily. Good connection from all above cities.

SEASON OPENS MAY 15th

CHRISTIES LAKE
LANARK COUNTY, ONTARIO

Red Cedar Inn 500 yards from Christies Lake Station C. P. R. Beautiful view of the islands from rooms. White sand safe bathing beaches. Ideal for children.

Three completely furnished cottages on the lake shore for rent by day, week, month or season, surrounded by an acre of land and shade trees. Running water in some of the kitchens. Good fishing in front of all cottages. 62 lots for sale, 3 beautiful islands, 3 camp sites, 3500 feet of shore line.

For reservations, booklet and photos write R. W. Marks, Prop., Christies Lake, Lanark County, Ont.

The best Fishing in Ontario— Small mouth black bass, pickerel, pike, sunfish, rainbow trout, perch, rock bass, whitefish, bullheads and chub.

Reduced rates for fishing. Angling License, $1.00 (one dollar), for three (3) days for non-residents. R. W. Marks, Provincial Game and Fish Warden, No. 120.

Boat livery, bait and licensed guides for hire. Free parking space for cars. Tent space for rent. Ice cold living spring water. Dancing pavilion.

Excursions daily among the 27 islands. 50c fare.

Daily mail, Bell telephone, C. P. R. Telegraph. Grocery store for supplies.

Motor Routs:—Montreal to Perth. Kingston to Perth, Ottawa to Perth, Brockville to Perth, Toronto to Perth and 12 miles to Red Cedar Inn, 4 miles from No. 7 Highway.

An advertising flyer for the Red Cedar Inn, the home of R.W. and May A. Bell Marks. Their son, Robert J. Marks, managed the inn. *Perth Museum Collection*.

A young Elton Crandall, son of Maizie, grandson of May A. Bell and R.W. Marks with his trophy from Christie Lake, circa 1920s. *Courtesy Elton Crandall.*

many of its islands. It is believed that R.W. started tourism on the lake with five rental cottages. The Red Cedar Inn, the home of May Bell and R.W. transformed into a summer hotel on Christie Lake, was later operated by his son, Robert J. Marks (deceased in 1988).

R.J.'s daughter, Maizie, whose earliest stage appearances were as a child actress with "Mom," married Elton Ward Crandall of Auburn, New York, and for twelve years operated a dance studio in that city. Maizie died in 1981. Her love of Christie Lake was passed on to her son, Elton Crandall Jr., his wife Betty and their three daughters who continue to cottage there.

Joseph Marks passed away in Perth on July 20, 1944, at the age of 82 years and 11 months. Joe's final years were spent quietly at the Christie Lake home he shared with his noted actress wife, Gracie. The former Mabel Grace Andrews of Grand Rapids, Michigan, moved into Perth following her husband's passing, where she resided until her own death in 1957 at 76 years of age.

The sudden death of Ernie Marks on June 21, 1952, truly closed an era of theatre, never to be seen again except for the occasional revival of a Marks play or skit. The youngest of the brothers, Ernie was considered the most innovative. He introduced the "kinetescope" moving picture machines in his live shows and pioneered the bringing of comic strip characters to the Canadian stage. Kitty Reynolds Marks starred in husband Ernie's touring productions. She was a gifted performer, capable of straight leading lady roles and equally comfortable with comedy. Kitty passed away in Oshawa on January 2, 1964

A complete roll call of those persons deserving of mention would appear not to exist, although papers found suggest that various attempts have been made to compile family history charts. Ernie Marks was so interested in his Marks and Farrell roots that he engaged the services of one of Canada's foremost genealogists, Brian Gilchrist of Toronto, to assist with his search for family information.

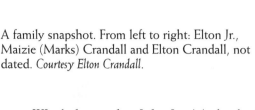

A family snapshot. From left to right: Elton Jr., Maizie (Marks) Crandall and Elton Crandall, not dated. *Courtesy Elton Crandall.*

We do know that John Jay Marks died in Tulameen, British Columbia, on December 22, 1939. He was eighty years old. Little is known about the final days of Alex Marks, but an 1881 census lists his year of birth as 1867. Records confirm his death in 1914. McIntyre Marks all but disappeared in Western Canada during the early 1900s, with brief appearances in the theatrical world. It would appear that McIntyre was born in 1871 and died in 1920 at 49 years of age. There seems to be some confusion around his actual birthdate, but none of it jibes with the 1881 census information.

One of the two Marks sisters, Olivia Mariah (Libby), appears to have passed away in 1916. The year of death for Ellen (Nellie) Marks would appear to have been 1934. She was married to Morley D. White, a contractor at Christie Lake. Neither of the sisters ever took to the stage, although they may have travelled with some of the families from time to time.

In this day of electronic entertainment and blockbuster Broadway shows, the old melodramas, so much a part of the vaudeville circuit would appear sadly outdated. But in the almost fifty successful years that saw up to five different Marks companies on the road, such entertainment as they offered could be great fun for the whole family. They knew that people liked to laugh and, as R.W. observed, "... the man who can sell tickets to a laugh is on his way to a fortune."[1] It has been said that one of the strongest features of the Marks presence in any community was the apparent gentility of the women in their companies. The Marks wives never drank liquor or smoked cigarettes. Their

A gathering on the porch verandah at the Red Cedar Inn. *Courtesy Elton Crandall.*

The Cole Automobile driven by R.W. Marks in the 1920s, parked in front of the Red Cedar Inn.
Courtesy Elton Crandall.

John Jay Marks spent most of his life in the Canadian West. When a Marks Brothers troupe, often Tom Marks and his company, headed for the prairies or beyond, the two brothers usually spent time together. *Perth Museum Collection*.

gowns, always glamorous and costly, both on stage and off, were frequently copied by many local belles. From R.W.'s perspective we hear the following:

"Over the lifetime of the Marks enterprises our people have absolutely refused to compromise on honest and orderly entertainment. Stock companies [like ours] most depend on family patronage ...."[2]

One cannot but marvel at both the stamina and creativity of yesterday's touring performers, stars in the days of the horsehair sofa and town halls transformed into theatres with their roll-back curtains. What fun it must have been to play week-long fall fairs, as well as Main Street Canada and USA opera halls! How gratifying it had to have been to offer up clean-cut amusement and wholesome entertainment geared to

Joseph Marks in his later years with his wife Gracie Marks at their home by Christie Lake.
Courtesy Elton Crandall.

delight family audiences, and guaranteed to bring patrons back on annual repeat dates, twenty and thirty years later. Small wonder that in a *Maclean's* magazine article dated June 21, 1957, Kitty Marks, on remembering her life with the original touring Marks Stock Company, summarized by saying: "I would gladly start my life with the Marks Brothers again."

No matter how minute or in-depth one chooses to analyze the careers of the Marks Brothers, the main conclusion quickly reached confirms a collective astuteness to give their audiences what they wanted. R.W. Marks spoke volumes when on recalling his touring days, said, "You might say that we were benefactors on the road to fortune."[3]

May A. Bell Marks made her Canadian stage debut with R.W. Marks and Company in a production at Ottawa's Grand Theatre in 1894. She never left, but went on to earn the billing of "Canada's leading lady." Photo by Loomis, of Watertown, New York. *Perth Museum Collection*.

APPENDIX I

STAGE PERSONALITIES FROM THE MARKS BROTHERS COMPANIES

Over the fifty-year span from the time of Robert W. Marks linking with King Kennedy to form the first Marks Company in 1876 to the mid-1920s with multiple Marks troupes on the road, hundreds of colourful entertainers plied their trade and were gainfully employed. Many were skilled performers hired to join the Marks troupes, while other aspiring performers came by invitation to Christie Lake for auditions in the off-season. If hired, they soon became part of the travelling families.

Annually, R.W. and his brothers were scouting for new talent and the next headliner. This collection of photographs is but a small representation of those performers of yesteryear who enthralled audiences across much of Canada and the northern United States.

Olive Byran and Frank Nelson – "just a dandy pair!"
Perth Museum Collection.

Dora Putnam in "Memories in the Sweet Long Ago" — a Marks production, date unknown. "Dora has my watercurl wig on," noted Gracie Marks in her own handwriting. Photo by the Hopkins Studio of St. Thomas, Ontario. *Perth Museum Collection.*

Dora Putnam, shown here, Madeline Ben and Gracie Purdue Marks played to over 1700 people at the Star Theatre in St. Thomas, Ontario. Photo by the Hopkins Studio of St. Thomas. *Perth Museum Collection.*

The Tom Marks Stock Company, 1915 season. Tom Marks, with his top hat, is standing in the centre of the back row. To his left is Joe Marks, with Gracie front right. *Courtesy Doug Bell.*

The singer, Madame Couttes Ban [?], and Mabel Grace M. Marks in a New York production, dated late fall 1913. *Perth Museum Collection.*

Madeline Ben and Dora Putnam in "Memories of
the Sweet Long Ago." This was the initial tryout
of this Marks Brothers production. Photo by the
Hopkins Studio of St. Thomas, Ontario.
Perth Museum Collection.

Gertrude Fox, 1914, described by Gracie Marks
as being "another good scout."
Courtesy Doug Bell.

Luella Breen in 1914, one of Gracie Marks'
stage pals. *Courtesy Doug Bell.*

Fred Dunn is described as "My Tutor" in an
album kept by Gracie. *Perth Museum Collection.*

This print was pulled on February 3, 1987, at the *Perth Courier* office from a copper halftone plate found in the Marks Brothers script bin. The subject is one of the members of the Marks Brothers Co., Wilfred Roger, playing Man – the Man of Mystery in the play "The Servant in the House." The photographer was Mallon of New York. The photo, dated May 1904, would have been used for advance publicity. *Perth Museum Collection*.

APPENDIX II

THEATRICAL MEMORABILIA

Thanks to the Perth Museum and such collectors as Douglas (Doug) Bell these rare reminders of the past have been preserved. In most instances, the playbills and other theatre ephemera shown here have been selected from a scrapbook meticulously kept by Gracie Marks from 1901 to the 1930s.

The photo albums kept by Grace Marks contain numerous autographed photos of many fellow performers, such as this cycling family shown here in a photograph dated November 21, 1914
Courtesy Doug Bell.

Program 1 (left)

SPECIAL ENGAGEMENT

MARKS BROS.

Dramatic and Vaudeville Co., with

GRACIE MARKS

Thursday Evening, April 11

THE PASTORAL DRAMA IN FOUR ACTS

"THORNS AND ORANGE BLOSSOMS"

By Joseph Vance

CAST OF CHARACTERS

Randolph Randolph	} Chris Chisholm
Lord Randolph Rivers	
Oscar Carston	Herbert McGurre
Patrick Brannigan	Jessie Sours
Ikie Cohen	Arthur Herbert
Antonio	Frank Grimshaw
Rev. Mr. Barstow	} Joseph Vance
Officer	
Kittie Edwards	Florence Thompson
Lady Rivers, Dowager	Bonnie Vance
GRACIE MARKS......as......Violet Lady Rivers	

SYNOPSIS

Act I—St. Phillips, on the Mediterranean. Summer.
Act II—Drawing Room at Riverswell, Kent, England, Fall.
Act III—The Mission, London. Winter.
Act IV—Rectory of St. Bynos. Spring.

UP-TO-DATE SPECIALTIES

will be introduced by the following artists :—G
Marks, Jessie and Beatrice Sours, Charlie Bank
Vance, Chris Chisholm and Jim Prim, Joe Mar
Marketoscope. Mr. Gerald Cooper, Musical D

Tomorrow Night
"VIRGIE'S SWEETHEA

Matinee Saturday Afternoon

*Beautiful white s
chiffon tunic white & blac
loyal beads edge
Pale bene satin a*

Program 2 (right)

EMPIRE

THE QUALITY PLAYHOUSE

SPECIAL ENGAGEMENT

MARKS BROS.

Dramatic and Vaudeville Co., with

GRACIE MARKS

Wednesday, OCT. 23rd.

The Pastoral Drama in Four Acts

"The Circus Girl."

JOS. VANCE, Director

CAST OF CHARACTERS.

Robert Gordon	Mr. Chris. Chisholm
James Arnold	Mr. M. A. Brewer
Joshua Gordon	Mr. Jos. Vance
Bingley Butes	Mr. George Morgan
Amasa Spencer	Mr. Ed. Mills
Dan Punch	Mr. Al Beckerich
Con Connors	Mr. Frank Williams
Jane Marvin	Miss Ellen M. Andrews
Sarah Chiffles	Miss Bonnie Vance
MISS GRACIE MARKS ...as...	The Circus Girl

SYNOPSIS

ACT I.—Interior of the Parsonage.
ACT II.—Exterior of the Parsonage.
ACT III.—Parlor in the Village Hotel.
ACT IV.—The Circus Ground.
Time.—The Present. Place.—A Village in the Middle West.

SPECIALTIES BY THE FOLLOWING ARTISTS
will be introduced :—Grace Marks, Jos. Vance, Chris. Chisholm,
Al Beckeritch, Ed. Mills, George Morgan, M. A. Brewer, Rena
St. Claire, Joe Marks and Marketoscope. Mr. Gerald Cooper,
Musical Director.

Agent, J. Clyde Fisher.

COMING:

Thursday Night, " The Bachelor's Ward."
Saturday Matinee 2.30, "Polly."
Monday, Oct. 28th, "The Third Degree."

WOODSTOCK OPERA HOUSE
Friday, October 28th, 1910

MARKS BROS.
No. A-1 Company

"Two Nights in Rome"

Cast of Characters.

Sir Horace Welby	Harry A. Starr
Barratto	Will H. Malone
Prince Malleotta	Frank Byron
Servant	Bruce Kent
Council	Will F. Crockett
Stephenie de Moraveaur	Elizabeth Fox
Alice Verney	Olive Nelson
Mrs. Foley	Kate Marsden
Rose Verney	Molly Starr

Synopsis of Scenes.

ACT I—The Serpent.
ACT II—The answer to a prayer.
ACT III—The Corsican's Revenge.

To-morrow Night—"A FAMILY FUED," or
"A DEVIL'S LANE"

Up-to-date specialties will be introduced at
performance by the following artists: Gracie M.
Bruce Kent, Elizabeth Fox, Byron and Nelso
F. Malone, Joe Marks and the Markettescop

Executive Staff.

Joe Marks	Stage
Frank Byron	Master
Bruce Kent	Repr
Mack Marks	Master of
Fred Deutrizac	Music
George A. Fox	

Prize Matinee To-morrow (Saturda
"LITTLE ALABAMA"

Grand Opera House
MEAFORD
Saturday Evening, October 15th

MARKS' BROS.
NO. A-1 COMPANY

"In Mizzouri"
A Great Western Drama in Four Acts

CAST OF CHARACTERS

Jim Radburn	
Robert Travers	Harry A. Starr
J. Vernon	Will H. Malone
Col. Bollinger	Will F. Crocket
Sam Fowler	Frank Bryon
Dave	J. T. Dutrizac
Esrom	Bruce Kent
Bill	Ed. Mitchell
Kelly	Art Hawley
Mrs. Joe Vernon	Joe Marks
Emily Radburn	Kate Marsden
Kate Vernon	Molly Star
Elizabeth Vernon	Elizabeth Fox
	Gracie Marks

SYNOPSIS OF SCENES

ACT I.—Pike County. Dining-room and Kitchen.
ACT II—Vernon's Blacksmith Shop adjoining his living room.
ACT III—Same as Act I
ACT IV—Exterior of Jim Radburn's Cabin

Up-to-date specialities will be introduced by the
following artists: Gracie Marks, Bruce Kent, Elizabeth
Fox, Byron and Nelson, Will F. Malone, Joe Marks and
the Markettescope.

VICTORIA OPERA HOUSE

Petrolia, H. ROTSKY, Manager.

WEDNESDAY, April 2nd.

MARKS BROS.

PRESENT

'The Girl from Sunny Alberta'

CAST OF CHARACTERS

Archy Wintrope	Al. Beckerich
Sir Blakesly Beresford	M. A. Brewer
Geoffrey Caryl	Fred P. Miller
Henry Weatherford	Ed. Mills
Wilson	Joe Vance
Lady Vi Beauchamp	Ellen M. Andrews
Ethel Osborne	Luella Breen
Priscilla Peabody	Bonnie Vance

GRACIE MARKS, as Robin Weatherford (The Girl from Sunny Alberta)

SYNOPSIS

ACT I.—Drawing room at the "Withercome Wold." Morning.

ACT II.—Same as Act I. Half an hour later.

ACT III.—The Terrace. Afternoon.

ACT IV.—Same as Act I. Evening.

SPECIALTIES BY THE FOLLOWING ARTISTS

Will be introduced :—Gracie Marks, Joe Vance, Chris. Chrisholm, Al. Beckerich, Ed. Mills, Fred P. Miller, M. A. Brewer, Luella Breen, Arthur Wilson.

High-Class Vaudeville Between Each Act.

SONGS SUNG BY MARKS BROS. CO.

"Bogie Man Rag "—Chas. K. Harris, New York.

"When I Get You Alone To-night "—Leo Feist, New York.

Prices---15c, 25c and 35c

AUDITORIUM, Fort William

Oct. 25 to 30

Marks Bros.

No. A-1 Co.

TONIGHT

"Brother Against Brother"

Matinee, Saturday, 2.30—
"Kidnaped by the Gyqsies"

Night prices—25, 35 and 50c
Matinee Prices—15 and 25c.

Star Theatre

GEO. O. PHILIP, Manager.

TUESDAY EVENING, MARCH 12th, 1912

MARKS BROS.

—WITH—

GRACIE MARKS

—IN—

"A Ragged Princess"

CAST OF CHARACTERS

Jack Merry, a Young Northener ....Chris Chisholm
Col. Robt. Silverthorn, a planter.........................Charlie Banks
Lee Silverthorn, his nephew..........................Herbert McGurre
Judas, his overeeer .... Joe Vance
Waggles, a tramp .... Jesse Sours
Juliet Silverthorn, his niece .... Florence Thompson
May Lou Marston, a friend .... Beatice Sours
Mrs. Biggs .... Emma Beame
Phoebe .... Bonnie Vance
Selma Silverthorn, known as the Princess ....GRACIE MARKS

SYNOPSIS

ACT I—Home of Col. Silverthorn.

ACT II—His adjoining plantation.

ACT III—The old boat house on the Bayou.

ACT IV—Same as Act II. Three years later.

UP-TO-DATE SPECIALTIES

Will be introduced by the following artists :—Gracie Marks,
Jesse and Beatrice Sours, Charlie Banks, Joe Vance, Chris
Chisholm and Jim Prim, Joe Marks and the Marketoscope.

Hear Miss Gracie Marks as The Ragged Princess feature Harold
Rossiter's New York hit, "Let Me Call You Sweetheart."

Mr. Gerald Cooper, Musical Director.

PRICES—10c, 20c. and 30c.

To-Morrow Night—" Master and Man."

*St. Thomas.
Ont.*

The Perth Town Hall, the centrepiece of downtown Perth, bears the date 1863. The context of many references made to this site would suggest that the Perth Opera House and the Perth Town Hall are one and the same. Here, over the years, many audiences were entertained by the Marks Brothers troupes. *Perth Museum Collection.*

PERTH OPERA HOUSE

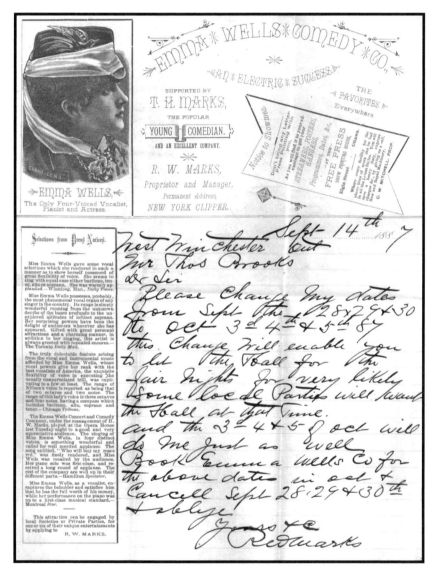

Late in August 2001, Susan McNichol, the curator of the Perth Museum, made an astounding discovery – a bundle of letters dated in the mid-1880s, bound together with twine. Obviously, they had lain, untouched, for many years. The letters are addressed to the Perth Opera House or the Perth Town Hall and are requests for bookings. Of particular interest is the one written on the Emma Wells Comedy Company letterhead, signed by R.W. Marks and dated September 14, 1887. He is asking for a change of booking date, from September 28, 29 and 30 to October 3, 4 and 5. R.W. suggests that this will allow the Hall to be available for some local parties during the Fair week. *Perth Museum Collection.*

APPENDIX IV
FAMILY TREE*

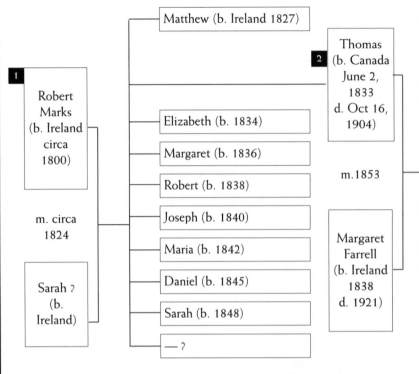

[1] Robert Marks (b. Ireland circa 1800)

m. circa 1824

Sarah ? (b. Ireland)

- Matthew (b. Ireland 1827)
- Elizabeth (b. 1834)
- Margaret (b. 1836)
- Robert (b. 1838)
- Joseph (b. 1840)
- Maria (b. 1842)
- Daniel (b. 1845)
- Sarah (b. 1848)
- — ?

[2] Thomas (b. Canada June 2, 1833 d. Oct 16, 1904)

m. 1853

Margaret Farrell (b. Ireland 1838 d. 1921)

- Robert William "R.W." (b. 1855 - d. Aug. 21, 1937) m. Dec. 16, 1898 May A. Bell (b. Aug. 20, 1871 d. March 17, 1932)
- Thomas Henry "Tom" (b. 1857 - d. March 9, 1936) m. circa 1886 Ella Maude Brokenshire (b. ? - d. 1931)
- John Jay (b. 1859 - d. Dec. 22, 1939) m. Jan. 17, 1906 Blanche Brown (b. 1884 - d. ?)
- Joseph "Joe" (b. 1862 - d. July 20, 1944) m. 1905 Mabel Grace "Gracie" Marintha Andrews (b. 1881 - d. 1957)
- Ellen Jane "Nellie" (b. 1865 - d. Feb. 26, 1934) m. ? Morley D. White (b. ? - d. ?)
- Alexander "Alex" (b. 1867 - d. May 18, 1914) m. ? (divorced) Margaret Anglin (b. 1876 - d. 1958)
- McIntyre "Mack" (b. 1871 - d. 1920) m. Oct. 31, 1910 Laura Margaret Korry (b. 1888 - d. Oct. 12, 1939)
- Olivia Mariah "Libby" (b. 1876 - d. 1916) m. ? John Hamilton (b. ? - d. ?)
- Ernest "Ernie" (b. March 15, 1879 - d. June 21, 1952) m. Aug. 7, 1901 Katherine "Kitty" Reynolds (b. Nov. 22, 1884 - d. Jan. 2, 1964)

---

* The Marks Brothers left a legacy of numerous magazine articles, newspaper clippings, playbills and other theatrical memorabilia. Interestingly, despite what seems to have been reasonably tight control of information released to the press, there are great variances in the ways that names are spelled and in the attribution of dates. While much effort has been given to try to ensure accuracy by checking multiple sources, some of those discrepancies still persist. The best that can be said regarding the dates prior to 1900 is that, if not precisely accurate, they are close. According to Toronto genealogist Brian Gilchrist, in a letter to Ernest Marks QC (Ernie's son) dated February 9, 1979, the gap between the actual taking of the census and actual returns usually meant that individuals were asked "What will your age be on your *next* birthday?" Should the person just have had a birthday, the response would throw the year out by one. He goes on to point out "... the rule of thumb is to say the [these] ages are accurate with a five year waiver, on either side."

As for the later dates, we are indebted to Katherine Kelly of Ajax, Ontario (granddaughter of Ernie), Ted Marks of Oshawa, Ontario, (grandson of Ernie), Harry Chesher of Penticton, B.C. (grandson of McIntyre), Rebecca "Becky" (Crandall) Smith (great-granddaughter of R.W. and May A. Bell) and Robert "Bob" Bond of Florida. For other background, you can visit Katherine Kelly's website, "The Fabulous Marks Brothers," at http://members.home.net/markswebmaster/.

Any additional information brought to the attention of the publisher will be rectified in subsequent editions.

DESCENDANTS OF SECOND GENERATION MARKS FAMILY

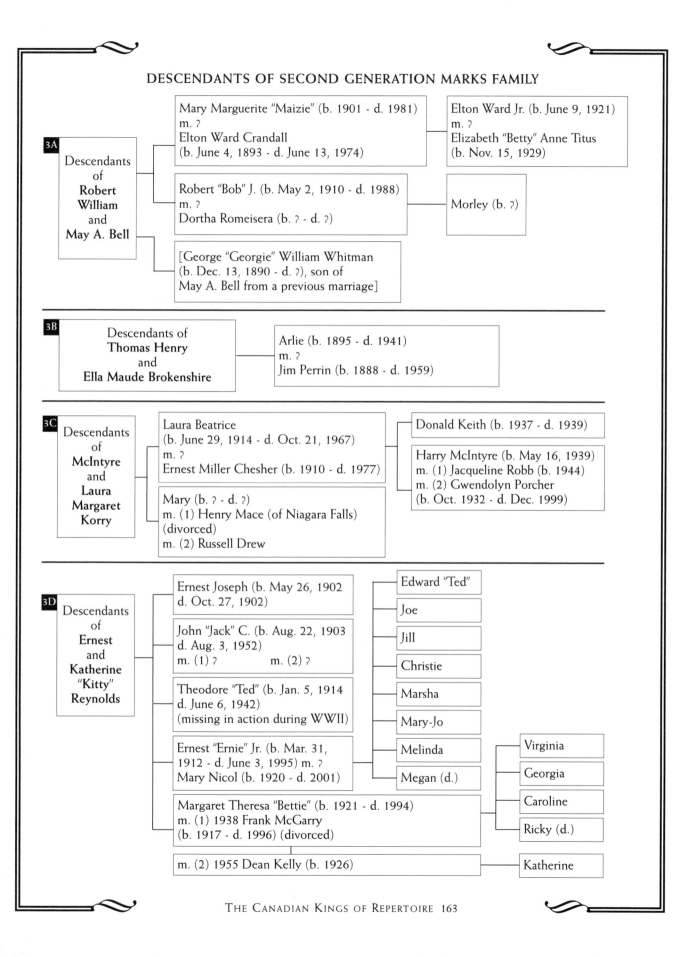

3A Descendants of **Robert William** and **May A. Bell**

Mary Marguerite "Maizie" (b. 1901 - d. 1981)
m. ?
Elton Ward Crandall
(b. June 4, 1893 - d. June 13, 1974)

Elton Ward Jr. (b. June 9, 1921)
m. ?
Elizabeth "Betty" Anne Titus
(b. Nov. 15, 1929)

Robert "Bob" J. (b. May 2, 1910 - d. 1988)
m. ?
Dortha Romeisera (b. ? - d. ?)

Morley (b. ?)

[George "Georgie" William Whitman
(b. Dec. 13, 1890 - d. ?), son of
May A. Bell from a previous marriage]

3B Descendants of **Thomas Henry** and **Ella Maude Brokenshire**

Arlie (b. 1895 - d. 1941)
m. ?
Jim Perrin (b. 1888 - d. 1959)

3C Descendants of **McIntyre** and **Laura Margaret Korry**

Laura Beatrice
(b. June 29, 1914 - d. Oct. 21, 1967)
m. ?
Ernest Miller Chesher (b. 1910 - d. 1977)

Donald Keith (b. 1937 - d. 1939)

Harry McIntyre (b. May 16, 1939)
m. (1) Jacqueline Robb (b. 1944)
m. (2) Gwendolyn Porcher
(b. Oct. 1932 - d. Dec. 1999)

Mary (b. ? - d. ?)
m. (1) Henry Mace (of Niagara Falls)
(divorced)
m. (2) Russell Drew

3D Descendants of **Ernest** and **Katherine "Kitty" Reynolds**

Ernest Joseph (b. May 26, 1902
d. Oct. 27, 1902)

John "Jack" C. (b. Aug. 22, 1903
d. Aug. 3, 1952)
m. (1) ?   m. (2) ?

Edward "Ted"

Joe

Jill

Christie

Theodore "Ted" (b. Jan. 5, 1914
d. June 6, 1942)
(missing in action during WWII)

Marsha

Mary-Jo

Ernest "Ernie" Jr. (b. Mar. 31,
1912 - d. June 3, 1995) m. ?
Mary Nicol (b. 1920 - d. 2001)

Melinda

Megan (d.)

Virginia

Georgia

Caroline

Ricky (d.)

Margaret Theresa "Bettie" (b. 1921 - d. 1994)
m. (1) 1938 Frank McGarry
(b. 1917 - d. 1996) (divorced)

m. (2) 1955 Dean Kelly (b. 1926)

Katherine

BACKGROUND TO THIS PUBLICATION

Much To Be Done is the most appropriate title of an insightful book dealing with the everyday lives of diarists across Ontario in Victorian times. The thoughts excerpted from countless diaries compiled by Frances Hoffman and Ryan Taylor constantly confirms that whatever one's station in life there was always "much to be done." Little wonder that recreation and escapism was so eagerly embraced by the many weary, hardworking individuals who on special occasions would find themselves entranced by the larger than life theatrical productions staged by any of the five Marks Brothers stage companies.

The publisher's first awareness of the Marks Brothers, seven in all, stemmed from my activities in the 1960s and '70s as a freelance broadcaster providing little-known stories to CBC Radio. Later, in the mid-1980s, while host, narrator and historical researcher with the syndicated television series *Sketches of Our Town*, I again encountered the Marks Brothers. This time I was on their home turf, filming a *Sketches* episode on the history of the delightful Eastern Ontario community of Perth, mere steps away from their personal territory at nearby Christie Lake. It was at this point that I became acquainted with the English-born journalist Michael Taylor, a reporter with the *Perth Courier*. Possessing a newsman's feel for a special story, Mike had already discovered the colourful Marks Brothers, subjects of many *Perth Courier* articles throughout the years. But it was not until the annual opening of the Rideau Waterway for the new season, when we both found ourselves in Smiths Falls, that Mike and myself more seriously discussed the idea of a book on the Marks family and their incredible careers as live stage managers and performers. Shortly afterwards contracts were signed and Mike Taylor began his work in earnest.

As any community newspaper reporter can attest, chasing fires, dialoguing with district police officials, attending and covering council meetings, plus countless other reporting duties leave little time for outside assignments. Thus it was that Mike Taylor's progress was sporadic and spanned several years, with this publisher infrequently receiving a chapter or a re-write and occasionally a work update. On those occasions when communication between Perth and Toronto became nonexistent, I would do the necessary chasing by telephone and, when called for, fit in further trips to Perth, in search of the author, by now an even busier individual as a result of his appointment to the editor's desk at the *Perth Courier*.

To his credit, Mike persisted, more updates and chapters arrived, eight chapters in all. But personal circumstances of major proportions came along without warning and Mike Taylor was no longer a part of Lanark County life. Not only had the *Perth Courier* lost a fine editor with his departure, but Mike's Marks Brothers manuscript was not quite completed. This reality led to the decision resulting in this publisher's written conclusion to what is otherwise Mike Taylor's book. Fortunately, Mike had made it known he wanted the book to move ahead and, to assist his publisher, he had placed appropriate illustrations in the Perth Museum, entrusted to his friend, the late Doug McNicol, then museum curator. Computer disks and a spare hard copy of his manuscript were also put in safekeeping, although the site was unknown to this publisher until almost two years ago. Fortunately, the whereabouts came to light.

The Marks Brothers always gave audiences their money's worth. They were special members of a way of entertainment no longer with us. But thanks to one Michael (Mike) Taylor, they return on the pages of this book for additional performances and curtain calls. These seven brawny farm boys from Christie Lake have earned a unique place in Canadian entertainment history. Because of Mike Taylor, their legacy remains.

Barry L. Penhale
Publisher

ACKNOWLEDGEMENTS

Many of the photographs and some of the information on the pages of this publication form part of the sizeable collection of Marks Brothers memorabilia and ephemera located at the Perth Museum, Matheson House, in eastern Ontario. The publisher gratefully appreciates the cooperation of the Perth Museum curator, Susan McNichol, and her assistant, Debbie Sproule. Further thanks are due to the many individuals who in recent years have donated or loaned Marks family albums, scrapbooks and miscellaneous materials to the Perth Museum, Matheson House, Perth, some of which has been included in this volume. Among these are Elton and Betty Crandall of St. Petersburg, Florida (grandson of R.W. Marks), Katherine Kelly of Ajax, Ontario (granddaughter of Ernie Marks), Douglas (Doug) Bell, John McEwan and Leonard M. Quinlan. Further thanks are due to Bob Sneyd, John Clement and Maureen Pegg for their valued interest and cooperation.

Finally, the late Doug McNichol must be singled out for special mention. No other individual did as much to encourage this work on the Marks Brothers of Lanark County.

NOTES

CHAPTER 1 – HOW ARE YOU GOING TO KEEP THEM DOWN ON THE FARM? 1876-1882

1. *The Billboard*, November 19, 1921; 49.
2. *Owen Sound Daily Sun Times*, November 1912.
3. *The Billboard*, November 19, 1921; 49.
4. *Perth Courier*, May 7, 1880.
5. Murray Edwards, *A Stage In Our Past* (Toronto: University of Toronto Press, 1968) 8.
6. Irene Craig, *Grease Paint on the Prairies* Vol. III (Historical and Scientific Society of Manitoba, 1947) 46.
7. Murray Edwards, 8.
8. *Toronto Star*, March 20, 1932.
9. *The Billboard*, 49.
10. *The Townsmen* (Time Life Books, 1976) 177.
11. *The Billboard*, 49.
12. *Ibid.*
13. *Toronto Star*, March 20, 1932.
14. *The Billboard*, 49.
15. *Ibid.*
16. *Maclean's Magazine*, No. 39, October 1, 1926, 17-18, 52-58.
17. *Ibid.*

CHAPTER 2 – ESTABLISHING ROOTS IN LANARK COUNTY

1. *Illustrated Atlas of Lanark County*, H. Beldon and Company, Toronto.
2. Private Collection of Ernest Marks Q.C.
3. *Ibid.*
4. *Ibid.*
5. *Ibid.*
6. *Ibid.*
7. *Toronto Star* March 20, 1932.
8. *Maclean's Magazine*, October 1, 1926, 17-18, 52-58.

CHAPTER 3 – CANADA BECKONS (1882-1892)

1. *Encyclopaedia Britannica*, Vol. 23, 1951, 13-14.
2. *Arnprior Chronicle*, October 5, 1884.
3. *Maclean's Magazine*, October 1, 1926, 17-18, 52-58.
4. *Pembroke Observer*, November 8, 1894.
5. *Listowel Banner*, August 20, 1885.

CHAPTER 4 – TOM MARKS - A KEEN EYE FOR BUSINESS AND A FLAIR FOR COMEDY

1. *Maclean's Magazine*, October 1, 1926, 17-18, 52-58.
2. *Ibid.*
3. *Ibid.*
4. Letter, dated October 20, 1987, possession of author.
5. *Maclean's Magazine*, October 1, 1926, 17-18, 52-58.
6. *Ibid.*
7. *Ibid.*
8. Article by Madge Macbeth, newspaper not identified.
9. *Ibid.*
10. *Maclean's Magazine*, October 1, 1926, 17-18, 52-58.

CHAPTER 5 – EXIT EMMA – ENTER MAY A. BELL

1. *Perth Expositor*, October 19, 1893.
2. Chad Evans, *Frontier Theatre* (Victoria, B.C.: Sono Nis Press, 1983) 135-136.
3. *The Billboard*, 49.
4. *Perth Expositor*, October 16, 1894.
5. Murray Edwards, *A Stage in Our Past.*
6. *The Evening Journal*, December 1, 1894.
7. *Watertown Daily Times*, December 7, 1928.

CHAPTER 6 – ROBERT WILLIAM MARKS – LARGER THAN LIFE KING OF REPERTOIRE

1. *Maclean's Magazine*, June 21, 1958, 58.
2. *Ibid.*
3. *Maclean's Magazine*, October 1, 1926, 55.
4. *Ibid.*
5. *Perth Expositor*, September 29, 1898.
6. *Watertown Daily Times*, December 28, 1928.

7. *Brockville Recorder*, November 31, 1898.
8. *Perth Expositor*, December 15, 1898.
9. *Perth Expositor*, December 22, 1898.
10. *Kingston Whig-Standard*, April 9, 1979, 11.
11. *Perth Expositor*, May 25, 1899.

CHAPTER 7 – LIFE ON THE ROAD

1. Sir John Martin Harvey, *The Autobiography of Sir John Martin Harvey*, XXXIX (London: Sampson Low, 1933) 428-430.
2. Interview with Bettie Kelly, April 8, 1988.
3. *Maclean's Magazine*, June 21, 1958, 17.
4. George Nelson Janes, "One Night Stands" in *Saturday Night* No. 51, January 4, 1936.
5. *Ibid.*
6. *Perth Expositor*, August 10, 1900.
7. *Perth Courier*, April 19, 1901.

CHAPTER 8 – PERILS OF THE STAGE BUT THE SHOW MUST GO ON

1. *Perth Courier*, not dated
2. Not able to identify source

CHAPTER 9 – HONING TALENT OVER THE YEARS

1. Not able to identify source

CHAPTER 10 – THE END OF AN ERA

1. Robson Black, "Ten, Twenty, Thirty" in *The Billboard*, Nov. 19, 1921, 49.
2. *Ibid.*
3. Not able to identify source.

INDEX